One Man, Many Tales, And A Separation: A Message Of Hope

By

James C. Birdsong, Jr.

Copyright © 1997, 2000 by James C. Birdsong
All rights reserved. No part of this book may be reproduced,
stored in a retrieval system, or transmitted by any means,
electronic, mechanical, photocopying, recording, or otherwise,
without the permission of the author.

ISBN NUMBER: 158721-224-2

1stBooks-rev.5/10/00

One Marriage, Many Tales, And A Separation: A Message Of Hope

About the Book

As you read ONE MARRIAGE, MANY TALES, AND A SEPARATION...A MESSAGE OF HOPE, you will be truly blessed by the many bible scriptures, testimonies and words of encouragement that truly gives all of us a message of hope. This book is more than about James story, it is about families, relationships, and encouraging us to go after our dreams in life if we always remember to placed God first. This book truly does have a message to all of the fathers all over the world, and their God given responsibility to be a father to their children.

We all need a message of hope in our daily lives that will encourage us, to inspire us and to lift us up with joy, and that message of hope is the Word of God. James was blessed with many responses in the book publishing industry about this book, including a book literary agency. It was a door opened from the Lord through the 1st Books Library to published ONE MARRIAGE, MANY TALES, AND A SEPARATION . . . A MESSAGE OF HOPE.

Acknowledgements

I give all of the honor and glory to our Lord and Saviour Jesus Christ for blessing me with a project that will truly become a message of hope, and a blessing to millions all over the world that truly believe in hope, and a message of truth. It's the answer after praying so much for a message of hope.

I want to thank my mother and the very best manager that her baby boy have ever know Belinda Germany Birdsong for her random act of kindness and dedicated work as a good mother. I am really graceful and I am truly blessed because you have truly encouraged me and supported the dialog of this book. I love you very much.

I have lost one of my relatives in 1997, and it was my father, the late James C. Birdsong, Sr. of Richmond, CA. He have departed this life on June 10th, 1997, but daddy will have a very special place in my heart, and that I loved him very much. I am continuing to move on what God called me to do.

I want to thank some of the many members at Emmanuel Apostolic Church in Vallejo, CA for their love, prayers and support towards me while I was visiting for a while. Stay strong and be encourage all the time, and God will continue to bless you like he already is if you always do what his Word tells us to do.

I want to thank my friends Joshua Bone, Samantha Mills, Fermin Maturin, Jr., Normaila Mills and my adopted play sister Kimberlee Ritchie for their blessful friendship, concerns, support, prayers and understanding towards me. I thank the Lord for you and always remember that you do have a special place in my heart.

I want to thank my former sixth grade teacher Ms. Donna Grove and her husband Ronald for their continuing, love, support, kindness and understanding over the years. You both are like a family to me, and I love the both of you very much. You two are special to me and God will continue to bless you like he already has.

I want to thank all of the teachers, administration and members of the faculty at the school that have truly supported me during the years at Nystrom Elementary School in my hometown of Richmond, California. You have always preached the message to your students about going after their dreams in life. Keep the message alive.

I want to thank Shaunte Bolden for her love, support and friend ship towards me and my mother. You have truly touched and witness to many people lives, and you have a very caring heart. Continuing doing the things that you are doing and you'll be blessed.

I want to say a very special thanks to the First Lady of Gospel Music Shirley Caesar (You are a inspiration to millions of people and I love you), Mrs. Coretta Scott King, Dorothy Norwood, Sharon Roberts and her family, Mrs. Rosa Parks, Dr. Maya Angelou, Malaco Records in Jackson, Mississippi and Tramaine Hawkins.

I continue my special thanks to Mr. Clarance Ivy of KDYA 1190AM Gospel Radio in Vallejo, CA, Rev. James Moore and The Mississippi Mass Choir, Oprah Winfrey, Dr. Bobby Jones for his popular Sunday gospel programs on Black Entertainment Television and the African American magazines Gospel Today, Ebony/Jet and Essence.

I want to give my last special thanks to my barber and good friend Bernard Delley of Eaddy's Haircare Center in Fairfield, California, Patti LaBelle for her beautiful autobiography "Don't Block The Blessings," Whintey Houston for sharing "The Preacher's Wife" movie with us, Fairfield High School, in Fairfield, California and to the best gospel in the Bay Area, Reids Records in Berkeley, California.

Dedications

This book is dedicated to my mother Belinda Germany Birdsong, in the memory of my father James Charles Birdsong, Sr., Sharon Roberts, my good friend and brother in the Lord Fermin Maturin, Jr., Alfred and Pamela Elbeck, Kimberlee Ritchie, Samantha Mills and her sister Normaila, Justin Ritchie and Aleah Elbeck.

The dedications continues to Lisa Strong, all of the historical black and Christian colleges in the United States, my good friend and fellow preacher Bishop Arthur Eames, my adopted aunt Kathrine Manning, the National Association for the Advancement of Colored People for more than eighty years of service, in memory of Martin Luther King, Jr., all of the many children worldwide, and finally in the memory of my uncle Roosevelt Daniel, Jr.

Table of Contents

Chapter One
Just The Beginning 1

Chapter Two
Moving On Up A Little Higher 9

Chapter Three
A Blessful Family Love 16

Chapter Four
Later On Down The Line 22

Chapter Five
From Family Love To Family Apartness 32

Chapter Six
Striving To Be Strong 40

Chapter Seven
A Family Love Breaking Up 50

Chapter Eight
Approaching A Separation 56

Chapter Nine
Into The Separation 63

Chapter Ten
Lord, We Are No Longer Together As A Family 70

A Message Of Hope 73

Selected Messages From Very Special Friends 75

Written Speeches By Evangelist James Birdsong, Jr. 78

Index 86

Introduction

I truly thank God for each and everyone of you around the world. It is a blessing and a honor to share my message of hope. Before I begin to share my story, testimony, and words of "One Marriage, Many Tales, And A Separation: A Message Of Hope," I will explain to you what this book is all about.

I also thank God for a message of hope because we all are going through in the last days and there are millions of people living in many countries that are hurting and crying for hope. I cannot stop thinking about our children because they are innocent.

In 1994, the Lord placed on my heart to write this book because I was thinking about the children around the world. The children of broken homes and bad marriages were the ones that were placed on my heart from the Lord.

When the parents of the children that are about to be separated or divorce, it really puts them in a mind of depression, getting bad grades in school, peer pressure, and even suicide. If a child is reading this book, then it will encourage them in some way.

Not only this book is about marriage, separation, and children, but it will feature major headlines that made history, education, relationships, familyship, and most of all, the Gospel of Christ in the Word of God because that is the real message of hope.

"And he said unto them, Go ye into the world, and preach the gospel to every creature."
St. Mark 16:15
My Best Of Wishes To Everybody
James Birdsong, Jr.

Chapter One
Just The Beginning

This story begins in the late 1970's as the 1980's was beginning to come it's way as the 1970's was a decade that had many history events. In September of 1979, a young woman named Belinda Germany Barb and her two sons Demetrus and Alonzo met a Richmond resident named James Charles Birdsong.

James lived in Richmond, California along with two other members of his family and they lived in a very large, two story victorian house that was built in 1914. His mother Charlene Walton Birdsong and his only brother Roosevelt Daniel, Jr. were the other members of his family that was living with him.

They were all from Greenwood, Louisiana and James and his family moved to the victorian house in 1968. While September was meeting time for Belinda, she also met Mr. Birdsong's longtime bestfriend Clim, his cousin Albert and his wife Barbara, many of his friends and neighbors and some other relatives. Belinda met James through a friend of hers.

A tragically all of the suddenly happened in the Birdsong family when New Years Day arrived. Mr. Birdsong's mother Charlene passed away on January 1st, 1980 of a heart attack. It left the family and the whole community very sad because Ms. Birdsong was special to so many people and she was very wellknown. She was very active member in her church and she was like a mother to a lot of people that knew her very well. Her funeral service was held at a church called Elisabeth Missionary Baptist Church in Richmond on January 5th, 1980 where the pastor Rev. J.L. Johnson did her eulogy.

Charlene was buried at Rolling Hills Memorial Park in the Hilltop area of Richmond that is about northeast of Richmond in a popular Richmond suburb called El Sobrante. About two months after Mother Birdsong died, her two sons were still going through the lost.

The lost was so bad that James and Roosevelt couldn't get enough sleep in many days. James and Belinda were getting married within a few days. On March 7th, 1980, they went to the wellknown famous gambling city of Reno, Nevada by car.

Three people went to Reno right along with them and these people were Paul, Diana, and her father. Her father went by the nickname "Pops" and these three people were accompany them to their little wedding that took them several hours to reached by car. As riding along the highway, the whole concept of the outdoors had heavenly beauty.

The concept was so beautiful that it was like the famous painter Leonardo Da Vinci painting. He became very famous for introducing his famous Mona Lisa painting. The snow covered trees were filled with heavenly beauty because it reminds me of all of the heavenly angels coming out of heaven singing "Joy To The World."

They went to the Washore County Courthouse to purchase a license for marriage on March 8th midnight and then headed over to Chapel of the Bells, a small wedding chapel that is a in and out wedding chapel. A man that was a wedding minister named Murrica performed the ceremony and James and Belinda's special guests seemed joyful about the wedding. Getting married is a blessing from the Lord.

After Murrica finished the ceremony, heaven rejoiced when James and Belinda became husband and wife and they were finally linked in marriage. This was the first marriage of James and the second marriage of Belinda. Mr. and Mrs. James Birdsong and their three wedding guests ate dinner at the Golden Nugget Hotel.

The Golden Nugget Hotel was a popular Reno hotel and the Golden Nugget was so crowded that night that security was getting heavy and it was more than one hundred people at the casino. The newly weds and their three guests were playing games at the casino.

Around six in the morning, James and Belinda Birdsong and their three guests start heading back to Richmond. The outdoors became life once again and it was like heaven opening up and the angels singing the gospel song "Love Lifted Me." In the afternoon about twelve o' clock, they finally arrived in Richmond.

Around March of 1980, Mr. Birdsong and his friends Irene, Carol, and some of his other friends gave Mrs. Birdsong a special party, which was a baby shower. She was expecting a baby and this child was going to be her husband's first and her third. Mrs. Birdsong was already six months pregnant.

Sometime during March, Roosevelt went to go live with his grown children and his grandchildren. The miracle baby that had talent and a very special inspirational career from the Lord was coming and Mr. Birdsong was uplifted with joy because he was experience to fatherhood for the very first time and this baby was a answer to Mrs. Birdsong's steps of motherhood.

On May 15th, 1980, the doctors decided that Mrs. Birdsong should be hospitalized for a few days. Belinda lefted ten in the morning to be admitted at a hospital. Heaven was rejoicing and the active doors of heaven opened up the next day on May 16th when a miracle baby of James and Belinda was born. There baby was a boy.

This beautiful baby weight was nine pounds and twenty one inches and he was born ten minutes after ten in the morning. The miracle baby's mother named him after his father, which was James Charles Birdsong, Jr. Mrs. Birdsong was hoping that her and her husband's baby was going to be a girl because she already had two sons.

Maybe God had his reasons for Mrs. Birdsong to have sons because any woman that have a son is blessed and should be happy. Mothers that have sons will be guarded and protected by them. The miracle baby of James and Belinda was born at Richmond Hospital, a former medical hospital that is now called East Bay Hospital.

East Bay Hospital is a hospital for people with sickness dealing with mental health and Mrs. Birdsong brought the baby home during May 21st, 1980 after staying six days at the hospital and several people and many more came from everywhere to see the baby. Family members were also pouring in from different places.

The Lord gave me a very important goal and task and that special goal is to become a preacher and to become a gospel singer during the later times in my life and I can truly say that is a blessing from the Lord and very intresting doesn't it? Months after months after baby James was born, people were coming over seeing him.

Albert's wife Barbara even wanted to take James Jr. home because she thought that he was so cute and beautiful. My father's friend Paul to be my Godfather and he was one of the three guests during my parents wedding. When a baby is born into a family, it becomes the most important gift that any man or woman can ever have.

Once the gift is here, it cannot be given back because a person can do everything that they can to give it back, but the special gift cannot be given back after God gives it to you for lifetime. Mr. and Mrs. Birdsong and their newborn baby would attend church services at Elisabeth Missionary Baptist Church on Sunday.

Since my grandmother Charlene died before I was born, my grand mother Mildred Germany was my only grandmother that was present. My grandmother Mildred was my mother's mother and children that have grandmothers are very blessed because they love her dearly and she loves them very much.

During the year of 1980, so many events made history and while 1980 made history, President Jimmy Carter lost to Ronald Reagan in the 1980 Presidential Election and the start of a middle east war between Iraq and Iran. A another event that was still going on in 1980 was the long Cold War between two powerful wellknown countries and they were the Soviet Union and the United States.

The Soviet Union and the United States first started this long Cold War after World War II ended in 1945 and when 1980 arrived, it was still going on. I am going to explain to all of you what the meaning of the Presidential Election is all about.

The Presidential Party in a Presidential Election is not a party that deals with food, gifts, and music. It's a govermnent party that have politicans such as representatives, state and federal speakers, governors, and other government officials get together and signed up to battle a certain authority in the government.

They run for the Senate, House of Representatives, and mostly, the President of the United States. These officials either run for the very first time or run for reelection and the truthful meaning of reelection is seeking a second term to win to their term according how many years they stay in their office.

These officials seeking to win will have "race wars" and they will have television commercials and other commercials against each other. These politicians will keep on having the race wars until the people of America vote on election day. After voting, then a certain group of people count the votes and make a news breaking announcement for the certain government office.

America have two main parties and they are the Republican and the Democratic Parties and the election only occurs every four years. A another event called the Olympic Games is a four year event that deals with sports. This event occurs in many places around the world and it deals with basketball, swimming, track and field, boxing, gymnastics and other sports that is feature on television, radio, and newspapers regarding people that are from different countries in different sports. The winning game metals is gold, silver, and bronze and the gold is the best.

Around 1981, my parents met a woman named Luzan and her daughter Rochelle. Luzan was one of our neighbors and she was a saleswoman (or distributor) for Amway. After they all met, my parents became Amway distributors for awhile, but not for a very longtime.

Luzan and my parents along with Clim became very close neighbors and the relationship between my father and Deacon Clim was family closeness. It's like when you meet a person and as you two become very close, then the both of you become a whole family. I believe that today and I truly thank God for friendship.

A friendship is designed to last a lifetime and the Lord planned this everlasting friendship. As we all learned about the meanings of life and the struggling to strive along the journey, I learned that if a person crosses their bridges of a special family friend ship, then that friend don't want to be your friend no more.

That special friendship went out of their way to give you things and to help you when your real family turned you down. The family love in a special friendship had broken and to give you a message of hope today about friendship, it is designed to last a lifetime and it's a blessing that was a match from heaven.

"A man that hath friends must shew himself friendly and there is a friend that sticketh closer than a brother."

Proverbs, 18:24.

This scripture about friendship is very true because it explains how a friendship is very important and gold cannot touch a friend ship because friendship lasts. My father was admitted to Richmond Hospital on January 9th, 1982 regarding a ulcer in his stomach.

He had surgery on January 12th and while in surgery, the doctors didn't find any major problems and it came up for them to reached a decision, so they finally decided for him to go home. My father came home to be with his family a few days later.

My parents and I became popular and people knew my father before he married my mother. The people that met my mother were longtime friends of my father. We had a lost in my family before my second birthday. On May 9th, 1982, my father's aunt Mary Birdsong Fields died of Alzheimer's disease at the age of seventy seven.

Alzheimer's disease is the disease that affects the brain memory lost and it usually affects elderly people. Usually when diseases such as alzheimer's affects a person, they will live at a resting home if they can't take care of themselves.

My parents had a problem that no parent don't want to experience or deal with. The Lord knew that the devil came on in and already messed things up with me, but I always been a happy child. Around February 1983, we was still going to church and praising God.

Since the Birdsong family is very large, they all have a Baptist background. My father was brought up in a Greenwood church called Greenwood No. 1 Baptist Church. My mother went to church services at Bethel Temple Pentecostal Church.

The late Elder Joseph Turner was the pastor of the Bethel Temple Pentecostal Church and she would attend services with his family and my mother wasn't brought up in the church and the Lord wanted my mother to do a special work for him.

Later on, we start attending Now Faith Church of God in Christ where Elder Robert Lee Crawford was the pastor. Since my mother was seeking the Lord into her life, she received the Holy Ghost on March 8th, 1983 on her and her husband's third year on their marriage, which was their third wedding anniversary.

Elder Crawford and his wife Mother Betty Crawford took Belinda in as a member of Now Faith and they knew that my mother really made the right choice in her life because we all are experience to the last days now and things aren't getting better. A person that is going through will say yes to God's will.

I already mentioned that my parents were having problems about me. By the time that I was three years old, I was a happy child that like to play, but I couldn't hardly talked fully and being born with a disability was part of the devil's plan. I was born with a speech impairment.

So one Sunday at church, Elder Crawford noitced something with my mother. The Lord showed Elder Crawford my condition and many other people knew what I was going through, so he had my mother to put olive oil on my forehead and pray for me each night that I went to bed.

After many prayers, the Lord healed me to talk fully just like everybody else and my parents were thankful that God came forth my way with a miracle. The Lord also gave me a voice of singing gospel music and the Birdsong family is a family that is gifted in singing and preaching.

My parents and other people were very happy that the Lord healed me to talk like everybody else and it is not only a pure blessing and a miracle, but it is a true wake up call for those who cannot believe that God can't healed and they should pay close attention to the many people that were healed by the power of God.

If the Lord didn't healed my voice to talk, then I will contunie to go through with the problem by dealing with it and it wouldn't be good at all. In the bible, a man named Moses that was a strong man that ever lived was speech impaired, but he had a true chosen calling on his life.

The Lord also wanted Moses to lead all of the children of Isreal out of slavery in Egypt after staying in slavery for four hundred years. Moses was going to lead them into a God given place called the Promised Land, which was called Canaan. Moses went up several days or more to the mountain top because the Lord was instructing Moses with certain tasks.

After I start talking fully, I start attending a Richmond school called Knolls Learning Center. It's a special school for children with disabilities when they are under five years old. Before Knolls became my school, my parents made arrangements to have the school bus called Laidlaw to come take me to school and bring me home.

I had two teachers named Joan and Sandy and I was in my starting stage of special education. I had fun at Knolls, but I was active and into the gospel more because God healed me. After the miracle occured, I was called into the ministry to be a preacher.

Chapter Two
Moving On Up A Little Higher

I was called by the Lord to be a preacher to preached the Gospel of Christ. Everyday in my room, I would have church in my bedroom by lining all my stuff animals while I was preaching. The animals were the church congregation and yes, I was having fun and having some church.

A lot of times when the Lord calls us to do something, we really don't be expecting that in our lives, but we don't have no choice but to say yes to the Lord's will and to his way. We must realize that our calling in Jesus Christ may become successful and values.

After I start attending Knolls, I met a boy named Ian and became very close friends later on. We both rode the same Laidlaw school bus every Monday through Friday and even though we went to school in Richmond, we lived in different places and we talked everyday.

I opened up my presents on Christmas day of 1983 and one present that I opened up was a Hot Wheels train set. It was the wellknown Freight Yard folding train set that made good sales. This popular toy set is no longer around, but I hope that it comes back during the future because it was a train set for all ages.

Even though I was going on four years old, the Lord was blessing my parents and I because we was into the church and we had people visiting us, even people in high places. My parents was wellknown in Richmond and had a lot of visitors from everywhere and several visitors from the church. Those early days were memorable because family love was growing strong and better. The everlasting loving memories are still around me and still in my heart.

So many events occured in 1984 such as the Presidental Election, the Olympic Games in Los Angeles, the murder of a Motown musical legand named Marvin Gaye, a civil rights leader named Rev. Jesse Jackson was running for President of the United States and Jesse became the first African American to run for president.

Other events that occurred in 1984 was the death of Martin Luther King, Jr's. father, the Rev. Martin Luther King, Sr. and a singer named Michael Jackson finally made history when became the "World Greatest Entertainer." He also made history when his 1982 release of "Thriller" became the bestseller of all time.

That year, Michael won eight Grammy Awards and the songs "Billie Jean" and "Beat It" are his hits from "Thriller" and are existing as hits today like they were in the early 1980's. He had hundreds and hundreds of screams at him while him and five of his brothers went on their "Victory" World Tour.

On January 16th, 1984, my great grandmother Floyd Germany passed away. She was the grandmother of my mother and she was the mother of my grandfather Otis Germany. My great grandmother was a person that had a lot of wisdom and knowledge based on real life, family life, and being strong.

She was the only person that stood by my mother's side regarding the time that my mother's family turned their backs on her during childhood. My mother was the black sheep of the family and people may think that I'm talking about a live sheep, but this different kind of sheep is talking about a person.

A black sheep is not a real live sheep, it's a person regarded as a disreputable or outside member of a family. My great grand mother Floyd comforted my mother very much and from that family closeness is a family love and it truly made her learned a truth in a lesson from her grandmother.

Floyd Germany was buried at the Sunset View Cemetery in a very small city called El Cerrito, California, which is at southeast section of Richmond. Around June of 1984, I completed my school learning at Knolls along with Ian because we was going to start preschool at a elementary school in El Sobrante, California.

Ian and I was going to attend Sheldon Elementary School around September of 1984. Elder Crawford died of a heart attack during 1984 and it lefted the congregation at Now Faith very sad about the lost of their pastor and their leader. He was a very strong and special man and I didn't get the chance to know him because I was still a baby.

After his demise, my parents and I became members of a another church called Faith Tabernacle A.O.H. Church Of God in Richmond where the pastor is Bishop George Washington Ayers. After being members at Faith Tabernacle in Richmond, my father was baptized and became one of the deacons. My mother was also baptized.

As I mentioned, Sheldon is located in El Sobrante and it still lies there. I had a teacher named Lynn and there was a everyday (Monday through Friday) teacher's assistant named Barbara. When I was attending Sheldon, I was still in special education.

There was a another lost in the Birdsong family. While opening up my Christmas gifts on Christmas day in 1984, one of my family members called my father and told him that one of our relatives died of cancer, which was our fifty five year old cousin Robert James Birdsong, Sr.

The funeral was going to be in Los Angeles and since my parents and I were going out of town to meet with the family, we decided to take a charter bus and since I didn't been out of town before between the time that I was born up to age four, it was my first time that I been out of town.

We boarded a Greyhound bus from Oakland, California and reached Los Angeles in about five hours. Los Angeles is the very largest city in California and one of the largest cities in this country next to New York City, Chicago, Seattle, and Dallas. My father's cousin George picked us up from the bus station.

George took us to his Long Beach, California home and we stayed there for the funeral. On December 29th, 1984, my parents along with myself and the rest of my family went to one of Los Angeles popular funeral homes for my cousin Robert's funeral. His funeral was held at Angelus Funeral Home.

While my family went to Robert's burial in Inglewood, California at the Inglewood Park Cemetery, my parents and I went to a church to wait for them. After they all arrived, my mother took pictures of my father and some of my relatives and while we all was dining at the church, I can remember eating some Kentucky Fried Chicken.

My parents and I left Los Angeles about one or two days later on a Greyhound bus heading back to Oakland. 1985 had many events that occurred around the world that made history. The war between Iraq and Iran in the middle east was still going on, the arrival of the space shuttle Atlantis and many others.

After World War II, there was a another war that went on, which was the Cold War between the United States and Russia (the former Soviet Union) and this war didn't had guns and missiles. Speaking about this war, it was still going on in the 1980's and continued up to 1990.

Michael Jackson made history again when he and the other members of the music and entertainment industry recorded a song dedicated to the people in Africa on starvation that had a powerful message of hope. The song "We Are The World" became a hit and it featured Diana Ross, Stevie Wonder, the Jackson family, and many others.

When I was attending Sheldon at preschool, the bus would dropped me off after school at the Contra Costa College child care center in San Pablo, California. My father had to go take a class called child development in order to keep me in the program.

I completed pre school in June of 1985 and I was looking forward for kindergarten in the fall. God really blessed us and my mother and father had their ups and downs and family love towards myself and my parents grew stronger everyday. One of my relatives became very sick, so my parents and I had to leave town once again.

It was my grandfather Jim Birdsong that we had to go see because he was very sick. My father was Jim's only son and was the former husband to the late Charlene Birdsong. We didn't ride the charter bus to my father's hometown of Greenwood, Louisiana to go visited my grandfather, we took a plane.

Albert took us to the San Francisco International Airport around the Burlingame, California area. We got on a TWA jetliner heading towards Los Angeles, then going to Dallas/Ft.

Worth on a jetliner of Delta airlines, and then taking one more Delta jetliner heading for Shreveport. It was like taking one flight to another.

After landing in Shreveport, I was kind of upset because I really remember accidentally spilling my honey roasted peanuts. I opened them up while the plane was in flight and before the plane landed in Shreveport, I can remember saying "airplane crash." This really made people on the plane nervous.

My greataunt Ruby Birdsong Jackson along with her husband Foster Jackson, Sr. picked us up from the airport. My grandfather second oldest sister was my aunt Ruby and this was my first time meeting aunt Ruby. My father was very glad to be at his hometown visiting family members and friends.

My mother and I received the chance to meet them and some family members remember me when I was a baby and some of them I remember meeting in Los Angeles for my cousin Robert's funeral. We brought along our camera to take pictures and a few days later, my father was glad to see his father.

My father was very glad to see his father because they reunited after eighteen years. I can remember crawling on my grandfather's bed and kissed him. A another time during our visit, my seventy two year old grandfather was admitted to the hospital. Jim became very sick and I met my great uncle Ed Birdsong, Jr.

Ed was my grandfather's last living brother and while my parents and I along with other family members was visiting my grandfather for a little while, uncle Ed gave me a bunny bank that had around several dollars in it. During our visit, my parents and I decided to stay with my aunt Ruby and uncle Foster.

Aunt Ruby and uncle Foster had a bunch of chickens and something about them attracted me since I loved animals. They didn't raised them for meat, they were raising them for their eggs. They really knew that I wanted to play and pet them and since I like chickens so much, I wanted one for a pet.

After the visit, my parents and I didn't fly back to the airport in San Francisco. So instead of flying, my father wanted a nation view of the states of Texas, New Mexico, Arizona, and the finally destination in California. We took a Trailways bus and I remember the outdoors was like a television program of education.

It was like traveling from a opened field to a large metropolitan city that had a Broadway movie premiere. I enjoyed the bus travel through valleys, mountains and hills, animals running in farmland and the sky being lighted up by the sun. Traveling through cities reminded me of a city lighted up at night.

Chapter Three
A Blessful Family Love

We finally arrived back home after traveling over one thousand miles on the road. I started kindergarten at Sheldon Elementary School in September of 1985. It was my last year and once again, Lynn was my teacher. While attending Sheldon for my kindergarten year, Lynn took us on a few class field trips.

On December 22nd, 1985, mama received a phone call that no person don't want to face. Her mother Mildred Germany died after having series of strokes. She was sixty seven and since I lost Charlene before I was born, Mildred was now no longer with the family.

She was my last living grandmother and she was also a wellknown person. She served as President of the National Council of Negro Women, members of the Parent Teacher Association of the Richmond Elementary Schools, the North Richmond Missionary Baptist Church Women's Missionary Union Society and a volunteer of the Richmond Rescue Mission.

A few days later, my parents and I along with my mother's three sisters (Glendora, Georgetta, Felicia) and two youngest brothers (Ivan and Daryl) and my grandfather Otis Germany attended Sunset View Mortuary in El Cerrito. My grandfather (who served in World War II as a United States Army drill sergeant) wanted his wife's funeral to be nice, private, and family only.

She was buried at Sunset View Cemetery where the funeral chapel was located. My grandfather didn't want my grandmother's funeral to have a eulogy or any music because he didn't believe in those kind of things.

1986 was a another year of history making events and a another busy year for my parents and I. The birthday of the late famous civil rights leader Dr. Martin Luther King, Jr. became law when President Reagan signed it as a national holiday in 1983. After it became law, it made Dr. King the very first African American to be honored in a national holiday.

Dr. King's widow Coretta Scott King worked for a very longtime to get her late husband's birthday to become a national holiday. She did received help from Senator Edward Kennedy to get Martin Luther King, Jr's. birthday as a national holiday.

Other headlines that was still going on in 1986 was the uprise of the Iraq/Iran War, the very long Cold War between the United States and the Soviet Union that started after the end of World War II in 1945, and many other events. A event that made around the clock news in 1986 that shocked the world.

This event involved with America's space program and it became headline news about the Space Shuttle Challenger. On the twenty eighth day of January (January 28th, 1986), Challenger exploded seventy three seconds and it killed all seven crew members.

It really shocked the world and the space shuttle program have been going on since 1981 when the Space Shuttle Columbia flewed into outer space for the very first time. One of the seven crew members that was killed on the 51L mission was a school teacher named Sharon Christa McAuliffe, who was one of the crew members on Challenger.

She was going to set up some lessons for the Teacher in Space project for her students. After Challenger exploded, all space shuttle missions were halted and the space shuttle didn't carry on it's flight to outer space until 1988. NASA was busy around the clock on a investigation about the Challenger explosion.

A another time in 1986, my parents and I went to a automobile center in Richmond called Hilltop Auto Plaza. The Hilltop Auto Plaza had Mira Vista Lincoln/Mercury and we was going to drive home a new car. About a few days later, my parents and I drove home a blue 1984 Lincoln Town Car sedan.

It was only two years old, but it still looked brand new with a lot of class. A lot of people, including at our church Faith Tabernacle A.O.H. Church of God though that our car was filled with class and the most finest car on the road. My father told my mother and I that we had to go out of town once again.

We had to go back to Greenwood, Louisiana again because daddy received a phone call from one of my relatives that my seventy four year old grandfather Jim Birdsong died of a stroke on the birthday of my late grandmother Charlene Birdsong. We all know that when we lose our loved one, then we must move on.

Instead of us flying, we drove over one thousand miles in our new car all the way from Richmond. It was like driving through a book filled with different places of interests, so it became a tourists atlas. My uncle Roosevelt came with us and he drove sometimes and my mother also drove sometimes during our trip.

We arrived in Shreveport about the next day and this time, my parents and I along with my uncle Roosevelt stayed at a house that belong to a woman named Clearne Norman, who knew my late grandmother Charlene and knew my grandfather Jim Birdsong. My father and uncle Roosevelt knew her when they were young.

On August 23rd, 1986, we attended the funeral services of my grandfather at Benevolent Funeral Home in Shreveport. I met my grandfather's two younger sisters, which were my aunts Gladys of Chicago, Illinois and Myria of Denver, Colorado. After many talks during the service, my grandfather was buried at Carver Memorial Cemetary.

After the burial of my grandfather, we all drove over to the dinner reception at my aunt Ruby's house. I wanted to see the chickens, so I went to the backyard once again to try to play with them. That evening, my parents and I went to go visit my uncle Ed and his wife Maggie Bell Birdsong.

He gave me a toy pickup truck and some other toys. We headed for the road once again to go home to Richmond. It took uncle Roosevelt, my parents, and myself over one hundred miles like it took us as we was coming to Shreveport. After we arrived in Richmond, I discovered something that really shocked me.

As I walked into the house, I saw all of my goldfishes in the tank dead and it made me very upset. It made me howled and so sad. In September of 1986, Ian and I finally started the very first grade, which was the first grade at our new school.

We start attending a school in Pinole, California not too far from Richmond called Ellerhorst Elementary School. Our teacher was a woman named Jean and her assistant was her longtime best friend Emma. A child have several blessed times in their lives and I am going to explain it in detail.

When a child starts kindergarten, the process of staying away from their mother and father rises. Later on, they will become use of staying away from their parents for part of a day. When a child turns thirteen years old, they are not only in a stage of adolesence, but having responsibility.

When a child turns sixteen years old, they are learning steps of going out on dates, driving a car, and having curfews. When a child eighteen years old, they graduated high school and the law consider them as adults, but the good part about it is the high school graduates are going to college.

So what I am trying to get you to see is that the first grade was one of the best times in my life. In June of 1986, Ian and I graduated kindergarten at Sheldon before my grandfather died on August 18th. In December of 1986, my father knew that I was asking for a dog, so he brought me my first puppy.

We went to a lady's house in San Pablo and after going to her backyard, she had a lot of puppies. The puppy that I took home was a mixed breed, which was German Shepherd with a another mixed breed or should I say race. My mother and I could never figure out what the other breed was.

I named my new puppy Tony, but I added "Wony" for his nickname. We had to keep Tony in the downstairs bathroom for awhile until he was old enough to be in the backyard. We gave Tony a blanket as he was inside of his box. So many events occured in 1987 each day around the world.

Michael Jackson made history again when he released his second best selling album "Bad". He was also going through a lot while people were talking about his skin disorder, which is a another skin color that is not your original complexion. The album have hits such as "Leave Me Alone," "Man In The Mirror," and so many more.

My parents and I lefted Faith Tabernacle A.O.H. Church in 1986 and we joined a church called Greater Faith Pentescostal Church in Jesus Name where Elder Jesse L. Ary was the pastor. The Lord placed it on my parents heart to start a food pantry at Greater Faith and it took some work to start it.

They had to go through the City of Richmond and other services in order to have the food pantry. Later on in 1987, my father's longtime bestfriend Clim went to Reno to married JoEvelyn. They came back and Clim introduce JoEvelyn to us. We all became very close in later years.

Two other members at Greater Faith knew that my parents worked to get the food pantry started and they also became a help with it. They were J.C. and his wife Mattie and just about everybody in Richmond knew about the food pantry.

On July 19th, 1987, the Lord called my father into the ministry at the age of forty nine. Before my father received his minister calling from the Lord, he was a deacon and he was a deacon while attending Now Faith and Faith Tabernacle A.O.H. Before my father was called to be a minister, my mother was called in 1986.

That was a blessing because not only my parents was a wellknown couple in Richmond, but they were ministers and their son became a preacher, but received his calling at the age of three. That's a very young age and that is very good. A lot of people couldn't stop coming over to the house and church while I was at school.

While I was at school playing around and chasing girls, Greater Faith and the house was the two places that held the food pantry and it was doing very good. Tony was a playful puppy and I loved him very much and he was growing everyday. We was having a major problem about Tony and it had something to do with a few things.

My parents would get into arguments about Tony and about buying him a dog identification tag with a identification number. There was a another situation about Tony and this situation was giving Tony his everyday walks. My father mentioned that the dog became the responsibility of my mother and I.

Tony was never given his walks by us and problems were building over problems and my mother had to go to the Contra Costa County Courthouse on thirty seventh street in Richmond and as she drove to court and back home over and over again, she had to do thirty two hours of community service until the fine was paid.

Chapter Four
Later On Down The Line

I found out about this story later on in my life and my father was blind since 1956 when he was eighteen years old. As he went hunting on thanksgiving day, a bullet accidently struck in both of his eyes as him and his two cousins were in the woods. While the situation about Tony was going on, things were going okay.

I would go outside everyday to the backyard to spend time with Tony and I loved him very much. He was a blessing and a special gift to me from the Lord even though I always wanted a dog that will become a another friend to me and there is a very truthful saying that a dog is a man's bestfriend.

The problem about Tony was so bad that the Contra Costa County Animal Services Department officer came out to the house. After the officer asked my father for his identification, he wouldn't give it to the officer. He made a clear statement for my mother to showed the officer her identification.

My mother had to do thirty two hours work of community service and she was doing it at the Souper Kitchen. It is a place where the homeless come and eat and a another popular Richmond pastor named Rev. Orenza Bernstine was the head official of the Souper Kitchen during that time.

In September of 1987, Ian and I started the second grade while we were at Ellerhorst again. I wanted a piano and I loved music, but it was gospel music and my parents knew about it. My father brought me a piano from a woman who lived in Hercules, a Contra Costa County town that is not too far from Richmond.

My uncle Paul came along with about two other men to help us with the piano. So the Lord blessed me with a piano and every day, I just couldn't stop playing it and I was going to learn to play the piano for a very low price, but daddy didn't want to except the plan for my lessons.

1988 was a year of events that was going on around the world and nearby communities. Events that made 1988 history such as the Olympics Games, the Presidental Election, Michael Jackson was on the world tour of his album "Bad", and the world's two most powerful countries were still having the Cold War and it was the Soviet Union and the United States.

I do remember 1988 and 1989 very well because they both were making history and many things that were going on at home and one of them I remember very well was about my father and Clim coming together to build a church. One of the beginning plans was to start having chruch underneath a carport.

The carport was at a vacant apartment that was right next to the house and it was going to be outside. A another plan that my father and Clim came up with was to have church at home in the living room downstairs. My parents and I stopped going to Greater Faith as members to join a another Richmond church.

My father and Clim tried to start a another church, but many things changed later on. My eldest brother Demetrus came from Los Angeles to visit along with his wife Vanessa. It was 1988 that they came up to visit and he was happy to see mama.

After the visit, Demetrus and Vanessa departed for Los Angeles and that was the last time that we saw them. Earlier in chapter three on page thirty two, I mentioned that my mother and father and myself became members of a another church in Richmond. This church was Apostolic Temple of Truth on thirteenth street.

The pastor of this church is Elder Vernon Robinson and a early time in 1988 on February 29th, a ministry that is a good partner ship with the United Way ordained my parents as ministers. This ministry that ordanied my parents is called World Christianship Ministries and it was during the evening.

This ceremony occured at Berkeley, California at the home that belong to a woman named Maple, who was wellknown for her gospel radio program on KDIA 1310 AM Radio. This radio station is very wellknown and one of the Bay Area's best gospel stations. World Christianship Ministries ordained my parents while we was still having church in our living room and outside in the carport.

President Reagan was the President of the United States during his eight year term and during the 1988 Election, Vice President George Bush was running aganist Massachusett's governor Michael Dukakis. The Rev. Jesse Jackson was also running for the second time, but lost to Michael Dukakis during the Democratic Party.

George Bush won the 1988 Election and took office as the forty first President of the United States in 1989. Ian and I started our third grade year at Ellerhorst in September of 1988. I like Ellerhorst very much and it became my favorite school.

I made a lot of friends and the teachers at Ellerhorst liked me very much and even though that I was there for three years until 1990, it will always be my favorite school. But none of my friends and classmates visited me and I felt lonely and my brothers were grown and out of the house, but my friends that lived close to me came to visit me and I visited them.

But 1989 marked the end of the 1980's and marked a new decade of the 1990's and 1989 was the year that I truly remember well because there was so many events that was going on that became history in the headlines. I also lost a special relative while 1989 was doing it's job and I will always remember this family member until death does it part.

The events that was going on in 1989 was the release of Janet Jackson's "Rhythm Nation 1814". It became a hit and her second bestselling album after her 1986 release of "Control" and 1989 was the year that the Cold War was still going on, the disease called AIDS (Acquired Immune Deficiency Syndrone) grew up very high since it's 1981 discovery and it was taking more lives.

The student protest in China's Tiananmen Square made national headlines for many days and even though that the United States and the Soviet Union was having the Cold War for so many years, the Soviet Union was going through many hard times. After 1989 arrived, KTVU Channel 2 in Oakland created Kidstown around the early part of the year.

I was so interested in Kidstown that I wanted to become a news reporter. I begin to write them in April of 1989 and I continue to write them over and over again. I had a birthday party after I turned nine years old on May 16th, 1989. I had my small party at school with my teacher and my classmates.

I am going to share a story with you about a man that I became very close to and I already mentioned that I had a lost in 1989. This book is being dedicated to the memory of this man and even though he only lived to see me up to nine years old, I remember him forever.

This is so hard for me to sit down and talk about because this man was my uncle Roosevelt. He was very special to his children, his grandchildren and he was mostly special to my father. Uncle Roosevelt only had one nephew and it was me and to give a truth of lesson to you, after all of the experiences that I had about deaths of special people, God still gave me strength to go on.

This lost of these special people were relatives on both sides of my family, friends, and loved ones and when they passed away, I truly thank God for his grace and mercy because it will carry you on with your life and I am a witness to that. It was around July of 1989 and it was about a week before my uncle passed.

Before July 27th, 1989, my parents and I went over to a church in Emeryville, California. It was a small church and after mama pulled up, we walked inside and we saw Clim and JoEvelyn. Their families and friends were also present in the services.

After church was over, I told my parents that I wanted to spend some time visiting my uncle Roosevelt and his family. The reason why that I wanted to go visited them because my uncle was really on my mind and I haven't seen them in awhile. My uncle Roosevelt lived in San Pablo and he was very happy to see us.

While we was over there at his house, I was talking and playing with my six cousins Equana and her sisters LaShanda and Lownisha and Aquatay and her brothers Alvin and Akenya. As I was visiting them, my father and uncle Roosevelt were in the living room.

They were in the living room talking mostly about my late grand mother Charlene Birdsong and memories of them as boys. My father talked to my uncle Roosevelt for awhile on the phone on a bright morning of July 27th 1989.

Later on in the evening, my parents and I became awakened after the doorbell rang. When my parents went downstairs, one of uncle Roosevelt's children told my father than he had died. When daddy heard those words, he was so shocked that he was speechless.

Uncle Roosevelt was only fifty five years old and after Denise lefted from telling my parents the news, my parents came inside of my room and woke me up so we can go use Clim's phone to call relatives. They told me that my uncle died of a heart attack.

I couldn't believe that my favorite uncle is dead and he loved me very much and I loved him. The neighbors were really shocked by the death of my uncle. My father was very sad about the lost of his only brother and my mother didn't had that much to say.

My father was very sad about his only brother's death and while we was over at Clim's and JoEvelyn's house using their telephone to call relatives and friends about my uncle's death, I couldn't stay in the living room, so I went to their kitchen and I really start to cry my tears out.

JoEvelyn came to the kitchen and told me that things were going to be alright. Daddy had to use their phone because before uncle Roosevelt died, daddy ran our phone bill high and the phone company had to turn off our phone until the bill was paid for.

After the phone calls, we start heading towards San Pablo where uncle Roosevelt lived and nobody wasn't at his house. We decided to go to the hospital in Pinole where uncle Roosevelt was rushed to, which was Doctor's Hospital. Denise's husband Mitchell tried to save uncle Roosevelt's life when he performed a popular first aid step called Cardiopulmonary Resuscitation after passing out.

After leaving the hosptial, we stopped by the home of Denise's sister Tommye and there wasn't no answer. We went back to uncle Roosevelt's house one more time and all of his family was there. My father still couldn't believe that his only brother was dead and he lost his mother in 1980 and his father in 1986.

Now since he lost his brother in 1989, the thought that really came to his mind was that he only had his son left and his only person that he had lefted was me. We stayed at my uncle's house for about three hours and we went home after midnight. My uncle Roosevelt's funeral was going to be on August 2nd, 1989.

On the afternoon of August 2nd, 1989 on the day of the funeral, my mother and I had to go to the doctor with my father. He told Dr. Brazell Carter that his only brother had passed and he also told him that he had to go to the funeral and preached his very first eulogy.

A eulogy is a special spoken or written composition about some body's life or character. My father was in a big rush to attend his brother's funeral, so we lefted the doctor's office heading back to the house so we can get ready to attend the funeral.

While we was getting ready to attend my uncle's funeral (which was held at Fuller's Funerals Richmond Chapel), there were some other people that came over to the house that was going to come with us to the funeral and it was Albert and Barbara along with his three sisters Mary Lou, Josephine, and Myria.

The eight of us lefted the house and went to Fuller's Funerals Richmond Chapel and my father finally preached his first eulogy and the funeral was a medium size funeral. Our Lincoln was very first in line behind the hearse of the procession to the burial at Rolling Hills Memorial Park out of all the cars.

After my uncle's burial at Rolling Hills, my mother and father along with Clim, JoEvelyn, Albert, Barbara, Mary Lou, Josephine, and myself came back to the house for dinner. Daddy asked uncle Roosevelt's children and grandchildren before we lefted Rolling Hills to come to the house for dinner, but they went to go some where else.

After the dinner, Clim and JoEvelyn went back home and Albert and Barbara had to go back home because Albert's three sisters Mary Lou, Josephine, and Myria were going to go home by leaving the Bay Area since they were visiting from out of town. I went back to Ellerhorst in September of 1989 to start my third year at the school and my fourth grade year.

I thought that Ian was coming back to Ellerhorst, but he went to a another school in Pinole called Tara Hills. My new school teacher was a woman named Laura and I was still thinking about my uncle Roosevelt everyday, but I wasn't going to let my lost of my uncle get in the way of my childhood.

Jean retired from Ellerhorst after she was teaching there for more than fifteen years and she was my teacher in the school's special education program from the first to third grade. I was still in special education when Laura was my teacher and being in it for more than five years really helped me.

It became a blessing for me and I didn't become ashamed while I was riding the school bus to school and being in the special education program because I had to learned to overcome it when other children would make fun of me because I wasn't like them and I had to overcome it after the 1983 miracle took place.

Before 1990 came, there was a another event that I will never forget because it made headlines and history and this headline took place in the Bay Area that became the famous Loma Prietta Earthquake and I am pretty sure that a lot of you remember it.

Before the Loma Piretta Earthquake hit the Bay Area that became front page news, there was a another event that made news during 1989. The Exxon Valdez oil tanker spilled more than five hundred gallons of fuel in the Alaska shoreline that killed most animals living in the sea and around the shoreline.

A another event that made history in 1989 was a wall in Germany that seperated the former East and West Germanys that was called the Berlin Wall that became to a end, China made headlines after a student protest in Tiananmen Square, and after flying in space for twelve years, the NASA Voyager II spacecraft made history.

Voyager II made history when it visit the planet Neptune, which is the blue color, eighth planet of the solar system. It retired from it's twelve year mission and it became the very first space craft to visit the planet Neptune. It's twin Voyager I completed it's mission in 1980 when it went to the planet Saturn.

About a week before October 17th, 1989 on the day of the famous Loma Piretta Earthquake, a another emergency happen to my father. His blood sugar was so high that my mother had to call emergency on him so he can be taken to Brookside Hospital in San Pablo.

My father was a diabetic and I learned that a person that fight this condition cannot be eating foods with a lot of sweet unless it was low sugar. After school, I was very glad to see my mother and I noticed that my father wasn't present. So I kept on asking my mother where my father was and she didn't say anything regarding my father until she surprise me at Brookside Hospital.

My father was hospitalized for about nine days and my mother had to learn about insulin, which she had to inject some into my father from shot needles, she also had to give him certain blood tests, and perform other medical activities. On October 17th, 1989, he was released from the hospital.

Daddy came home to be with his family and I was happy to see him again after nine days. That very same afternoon, I wanted to go outside in the front yard and talk to Troy, who was one of my neighbors and one of my closest friends. A another very close friend that I had was a girl named Tierra and she lived right next door to me.

She was like a sister to me and her family was very close to me while I would go visited them everyday and I was also very close to Troy's family, so all three of us lived next door to each other. While Troy and I was talking, my father turned on the television and was listening to the World Series baseball game between the Oakland A's and the San Francisco Giants.

My mother was outside talking to Clim and JoEvelyn and after while, then a earthquake shooked the whole Bay Area. The news came on and the World Series baseball game had to be stop for the breaking news.

The earthquake did a lot of damage and some of them were the Cypress Freeway in Oakland killing a lot of people after they were still on the freeway, the Bay Bridge's upper deck became a disaster after a section of it fell into the lower deck.

A woman that was driving on the Bay Bridge was killed and when her family heard about it, it lefted them into a very sad grief. The World Series game at San Francisco"s Candlestick Park cause many people running for their lives when some big rocks fell. Fires broke out in three Bay Area counties and they were Santa Cruz, San Francisco, and Santa Clara counties and the newsmedia were reporting that some more fires broke out, more deaths were reported, the electric and water supply had to be turn off when the newsmedia couldn't stop reporting this deadly earthquake.

In the bible, Jesus declared something that is very true about many today's world problems and the times that we all are going through in these very last days. There will be many earthquakes, violence, and many other things. That is what Jesus was telling us in the Word of God.

It was in the Lord's doing that cause this earthquake to cause a big damage in the Bay Area. Sometimes when the newsmedia work on a major newsbreaking story such as a earthquake, flood, fire, riot, hurricane, and other major disasters, a thought will come to their mind about why this is happening.

But they don't realize that it's in the Lord doing and through his eyes, he is getting tired of people doing things that don't represent good deeds and he is getting tired of people treating the saints bad instead of good and I <u>am</u> a living witness to that because you must be careful how you treat people and the reason why that I said that because you don't know who they are.

Chapter Five
From Family Love To Family Apartness

This earthquake made a lot of people homeless after this event destroyed many homes and buildings. While the earthquake really became a disaster, a BART (Bay Area Rapid Transit) train became stuck inside of a San Francisco Bay underwater tunnel that BART trains travel in everyday called the Transbay Tube.

The train became stuck after it was on the way to West Oakland where a BART station is located. On the night of the earthquake, a lot of my neighbors along with many family and friends lefted the inside of their homes and remain outside when the many fire and police officials were responding to emergency calls.

While we were all outside, a woman came up to my mother asking her to pray for her baby and my mother and my father's longtime bestfriend Clim prayed for her baby. This earthquake was second to the worst one since the famous 1906 earthquake that shooked San Francisco and it became history.

More and more newsmedia, firefighter and police officials with some other agencies were out reporting more stories and helping many victims. One month after the Loma Piretta Earthquake, many things were healing up and the Bay Bridge opened up after being close to the repairs to the section of the upper deck.

But the rest of 1989 was a history page filled with many pages regarding the Loma Piretta Earthquake. 1989 was closing because the 1980's and opening up to the 1990's and the eighties remain a decade that was filled with history that will never be forget by those who remember it well.

1990 was a another year that had a lot of events that became history and since it marked a new decade that made technology, it was going to be different. A boy that was in the headlines named Ryan White died of AIDS after battling with it after he received the disease from a blood transfusion.

Ryan was in the headlines in the eighties while dealing with the disease and the other events that occured in 1990 was the end of the Cold War, Nelson Mandela was finally released from prison in South Africa after serving twenty seven years, and he made history later in 1994 when he was elected South Africa's very first black president.

Other events followed such as Janet Jackson's "Rhythm Nation" World Tour, NASA launched two spacecraft in 1989 that were on their way to their targets called Magellen and Galileo and so many people were still healing from the 1989 earthquake. 1990 was like a continuation of 1989 and the events from 1989 were going on in 1990.

A woman named Kim of KTVU Kidstown in Oakland already mailed me two letters regarding me being a reporter for Kidstown and she wrote me for the third time asking me to come on down for a interview on Sunday, January 28th, 1990.

After we arrived at the KTVU Channel 2 newsstudio in Oakland, we had to go wait in the waiting room and while we was in the waiting room, I was extremely nervous about the interview and a few minutes later, Kim called us in for the interview.

During the interview, I felt more nervous because I was sitting at the newsdesk reading the papers in front of me while a camera was still going, but I wasn't on television broadcasting because it seem like that I was going to be on television and I wasn't.

Later on after the Kidstown interview, we went back to Richmond and Kim told us that she would keep in touched about me becoming a KTVU Kidstown newsreporter, but she never did. I truly believe that I was going to become one of the reporters and we all truly remember that the Lord have something better for us.

My parents and I didn't attend church services because we drove to Oakland for the Kidstown interview. I begin to noticed things in my parents marriage that wasn't right and these things during my parents marriage was still occuring before my uncle Roosevelt died in 1989.

I am talking about my parents arguing over things such as bills, my mother not talking to certain people that knew my daddy while he was still getting settled in Richmond in 1968 and while these things were going on, my father was talking about that my mother was not a good mother to me and not taking care of me.

Even though my father was saying that my mother was not keeping up with her motherly tasks of motherhood, my father wasn't doing his tasks of fatherhood towards his only child. I was very close to my father from the time that I was three years old and things all the suddenly changed. Even though that daddy lost his vision and was a diabetic, he wasn't spending enough time with me.

What I am talking about that my father wasn't spending enough time with me is the time that a father should spend the father/son time with his son by listening to him and teaching him the ways to manhood because every boy deserves a father and having a son for a father is a blessing from the Lord.

I noticed nowdays that a lot of fathers don't stay around for his sons and it's leaving the mothers to be the mother and the father to her son and later on in the boy's life, he will tell a person that something is missing in my life and he loves his mother, but it's not enough to guide my footsteps to manhood.

My parents joined a nonprofit organization in 1989 called the Shepherd's Way, a organization that goes around and help people that are using drugs by helping them to Christ and getting the people off of drugs, but they were being treated. This program was located in San Pablo.

Also during the time that my parents marriage was having it's time of difference, my father also told people that he was not married to my mother and that really put her down because this family love that was being touched by the Lord was falling out to the drain very slow.

Around February 1990, the NASA spacecraft Galileo flew by the planet Venus. Galileo was launched in October of 1989 and it's mission was to go to the big planet Jupiter on a six year long journey. Instead of Galileo flying straight to Jupiter, it had to make a few flybys on it's journey for a gravity assistant.

Galileo had to make one flyby of Venus, two of Earth, and two asteroids in the Asteroid Belt between Mars and Jupiter. Galileo was going to arrived at Jupiter in December of 1995. I enjoyed Ellerhorst very much and it was my favorite school. I attended Ellerhorst for three years and I took home many awards.

While I was attending summer school in July of 1990, I caught a childhood sickness called the chicken pox. I stayed home for a while because I had bubble like bumps all over my body. This really made me feel bad, but the Lord healed me for good.

My doctor had to give me a very strong lotion for chicken pox, bug bites, and poison ivy called Calamine Lotion. It dries the bumps and bites from these sickness on your skin. That was the very first time that I caught the chicken pox.

My mother had to put the lotion on me everyday until I became well again and after the Lord healed me, I went back to summer school at Valley View Elementary School in El Sobrante. Before September of 1990 came, the NASA spacecraft Magellen that flew away from earth in May of 1989 arrived at Venus on August 10th for a two hundard forty three earth day mapping mission.

I didn't go back to Ellerhorst because I had to attend school close to where I lived. I had to attend a school that was very close to my house called Nystrom Elementary School. The school was right across the street from my house. Nystrom is a school that have mostly black students attending and to tell you this, it wasn't my type.

It wasn't the Nystrom school building that was the main problem, it was some of the students and from that time that I was around three years old, I attended school in the white communties until I start attending a all black school for the first time.

My new teacher was a man named Douglas and his aide was a woman named Wanda. Even though that this class was a special education class, some of the boys in my class was making fun of me because I was different and some of them were also picking at me.

I was so hurt that I wanted to leave the school and some people were also saying that I talked like a girl and my parents pulled me out from Nystrom for a few weeks so I can go attend my former school Ellerhorst again. I had to go back to Nystrom and Douglas and my classmates were wondering where I been.

While I was at Nystrom, God was using me to preached the Gospel to everybody and I was noticing that a lot of the students truly wanted me to be their friend and a lot of the girls at my school had the upmost respect towards me and they admired me.

They all listened to me and some of the boys were still teasing me and they were very jealous of me. Some of the young men truly knew that the girls liked me very much and the girls were really concern about me sometimes, so they were watching out for me.

On December 8th, 1990, the spacecraft Galileo made a very first flyby of the Earth and the moon. It will make it's second flight of the earth and the moon on December 8th, 1992. After I started the fifth grade, my father decided to get him a home provider.

During September of 1990, my father's home provider was a woman named Shirley and her job was to take him places, give him blood tests, cook his breakfast and other meals, give him his everyday insulin because he was a diabetic and clean up after him. During that time, the tales of my parents marriage was getting worser.

It was so bad that my father was going around and doing certain things behind my mother's back and when he was doing that, daddy also did something that really hurted my mother and I, but after it ended, I had to let it go and move on because God wants every person to forgive those who did us wrong.

A lot of people that been knowing my parents started to noticed many things that was happening in my parents marriage and things grew worser and the tales grew worser. While the problems within my parents marriage grew, they stopped attending church services together as husband and wife.

My mother start going to church at Prayer House Apostolic Faith Church in Oakland along with her friend Adella, who was a friend from childhood and Adella's husband David also attended services at Prayer House. The pastor of Prayer House in Oakland is Bishop Presley Mobley.

My father was still a member of Apostolic Temple of Truth while my mother was at Prayer House and more problems grew while going to different churches in different cities. My father also didn't want me to go to church with my mothers and I would cried. After the marriage became many tales, I became a victim of confusion.

Before I get into the second testimony of this message of hope, my mother brought me a brand new bicycle on December 25th, 1990. The bicycle was my very first bicycle that I ever had and there was only one problem, I didn't know how to ride it and I really wanted to learn how to ride it.

My mother taught me how to ride my bicycle over at the Nystrom school grounds and at first, I thought that I wasn't going good and never going to learn how to ride it because I fell off over and over again and my mother knew that I can ride it after keep falling off to the ground.

She told me that I was a professor and I can do it and I tried riding it again one more time and I kept on going and my mother was right because it stayed with me up to this very day. During the time that my parents marriage became many tales, I was also going through many hard times and I already mentioned that this made me a victim of confusion.

Since the Lord is having me to share this message of hope with all people in the United States and around the world, sometimes I can go back and thank the Lord that I didn't go over the edge of I wanted to do when I was around ten years old.

While my parents marriage were many tales, my father was going around and doing things behind my mother's back and while these things was going on, he also did something that not only hurted me, but it hurted my mother because it involved us both. People were opening up to my mother and telling her certain things.

These people were telling my mother about some of the things that my father was doing before he met my mother. Every month, my parents and I would get money that we were recieving about the first of the month and all of the suddenly, my father got a hold to our money and he had full control of it.

It made us very upset and not able to get anything, not even food on the day that the money was issued. It was so bad that I would cried out to my mother because I didn't have anything to eat and how daddy was treating me. When daddy would forced me to go with him to a Lucky's grocery store, he embarrassed me in front of everybody.

I would asked him for a another item, but he said "No" after he would only buy me one box of cereal. This made me a victim of confusion and there is something else along with that made me a victim of confusion even though it's hard, but it really will help somebody.

I wanted to die very bad and I would even pray and asked God to take me because I was getting tired of the things that put me through a lot and how my father had changed and how he was treating me and not being a real husband to his wife by being a real man by taking up for her.

I wanted to commit suicide and I was tired of being hurt, sad all the time, being a victim of the abuse and I became really tired of picking between my mother and father and that made me a victim of confusion.

After my mother found out about it, she told me that I should not do that because I would've regret that and I wouldn't stay here today and I wouldn't be sitting down writing this message of hope. My mother decided that the money that we be receiving every month should be out of daddy's hands.

She took care of the business as soon as possible and it made me not take my life and after my mother claim the once a month money back, then she decided to get a part time job as a nurse for in home care from Jobs for Seniors. 1991 was not only made history, but it was the longest year that I remember very well and I was still going through a lot.

The events that was happening in 1991 that made headlines was the fall of the Soviet Union in their time of sorrow and tests when Mikhail Gorbachev was in office as the Soviet Union prime minister (president) from 1985 to 1990 and the start of a war that was going on between the United States and Iraq.

President Bush told Saddam Hussein that he should be out from Kuwait by midnight on January 15th, 1991 and this really begin to happen in 1990 when Saddam invaded Kuwait. The other events that occurred in 1991 was the death of the King of Gospel Music Rev. James Cleveland after battling with AIDS.

Michael Jackson recorded a another album that became a seller called "Dangerous" and after the Gulf War broke out on January 15th, a another relative died in my family and it was my great aunt Ruby Birdsong Jackson. She was eighty three years old.

Chapter Six
Striving To Be Strong

The cause of aunt Ruby's death was a heart attack and my father gave me the news after he recieved a phone call. Sometime during January of 1991, Clim and JoEvelyn were building a church before 1991 arrived and they finally opened up the doors of their small church, which is called Holy Mission Christian Center.

After they opened up their church in Richmond, my father wanted me to go attend services there one Sunday and we join the church about two months later after they opened up the doors. The doors were to christian experience or candidate for baptism.

My father became one of the ministers at Holy Mission and while he was sitting at the pulpit, I was singing in the choir because I always loved to sing even though I was very shy from the times that I was between five to about nine years old and I was mostly camera shy when it comes to taking school pictures.

The choir rehearsals at Holy Mission would be in the afternoons every Saturday and while my father and I were attending services at Holy Mission, my mother continue to attend Prayer House along with Adella and David and the marriage was still having problems with many tales.

Every Wednesday night, I would go to bible study and on Fridays, I would go to evangelistic night services. I was at home sitting in the living room and my father was telling me that I was going to be baptized one Sunday without telling me and I was extremely scared because I was already going through a lot and I was going through something else.

I was extremely scared and nervous because I was going through a lot and I was a victim of confusion. I was ten years old when my father told me about me getting baptized and a boy or a girl that is ten years old is old enough to make their own decisions about certain things in life.

I was very hurt because my father didn't want to sit down with me and asked me how do I feel about it and if I was ready.

When the baptism was coming up, my mother knew about it and she told me that I had to pray and to be strong.

I am going to pray and hope that no child be pressure by their parents into something that they are not ready to face. Instead of that, the parents should asked them if they are really ready to experience something instead of the parents telling the many children that they are because you must remember something that our children want and they have needs to just like you.

On the Sunday of the baptism, I was feeling very nervous about it and when it was my turn to go up to be baptized, I was asked some questions and some of them were if I believe that the Lord Jesus is my Lord and Saviour and many others.

So I went into the baptism pool and wearing a white robe while my father wanted to do the words of baptism. He went up to pray and said the baptism words while Clim and a man that was a Holy Mission minister named L.C. were in the pool. My father continue on after the prayer and said the baptism words when he mentioned "I baptized you in the name of Jesus Christ" for my baptism.

I was very upset that I wanted to cry and run to the back of the church, but my mother told me that I had to be strong and pray and that's why I didn't cry. All of the many things that I was going through of the way that my father was treating me and the marriage not getting any better.

Before my eleventh birthday came on May 16th, 1991, my class went on a field trip to a wellknown educational center called the California Academy of Sciences in San Francisco. We went to the planetarium and the aquarium. I was more happy when we went to the planetarium because my teacher and classmates knew that I was into astronomy and very good at it.

After we came back from San Francisco, I taught a class about astronomy and this special education class was a another class that went along with Douglas class to San Francisco. They were asking me about the solar system and I didn't stay for long.

By the time that I came back to my class, they really shocked me when they howled out surprise. My teacher gave me a birthday party on my eleventh birthday and it was my very first surprise birthday party. I wasn't expecting that and I made a statement when I said "Don't do this to me ever again".

They all laughed when I said that and the birthday turned out to be a unforgetable birthday and I thank God for that because it was a blessing for me. My mother gave me a another birthday party on a Saturday and since I had a very large birthday cake, my mother told me that I can invited as many people as I want.

The birthday cake was a strawberry and lemon side by side favor Teenage Mutant Ninja Turtle cake that served up to three hundred people and I was also serving potato chips, tuna fish sandwiches, vanilla ice cream, and soda. My mother was taking pictures while the party was going on.

The only people that came to my birthday party were my longtime friend Ian and my four classmates named Lawson, Clarence, Marion, and Jonathan. I did received some gifts and I was playing gospel music during the party. My prayers were finally answered because I always wanted to go to this special place.

My father and I was talking to me one day and as he was talking, he told me that he was going to take me to Disneyland, a popular amusement park in Anahaim, California that is very famous. Every child perhaps in the United States wants to go to Disneyland.

My father wanted to fly to Orange County, a Southern California county that is south of Los Angeles County and my father brought up that we was going to drive to Long Beach to spend the weekend with my cousin George. A man named Arnold drove us to Long Beach in the blue Lincoln Town Car and he was a friend to my father.

I really missed my mother while I was gone and we was traveling through Central California and if you ever drive through Central California, it is mostly farmland and there is a lot of electric power lines down there carrying electricity to and from Southern California up to Northern California. After staying at a resting place for a night, we arrived in Los Angeles in the morning.

We stopped at a few telephone booths to call my cousin George's brother Lee Arthur. I took some pictures with George, Lee Arthur, and my father when my parents and I went to Robert James funeral in 1984 in Los Angeles. Arnold did a lot of driving around while we was looking for Lee Arthur's apartment and we finally arrived at his luxury apartment at a senior citizens complex.

Lee Arthur was very glad to see us and while waiting for George at Lee Arthur's apartment, we was waiting for a few hours. After waiting for a few hours for George to leave work, George finally came over to take us to his Long Beach apartment. After my daddy and I came up to the guest bedroom, a woman that was my cousin's fiance walked in.

Her named was Cindy and after we met her, they took my father, Arnold, and myself out of dinner. They took us to a restaurant and while we was at eating at an all you can eat restaurant, mama was still on my mind. After dinner was over, Cindy went home and we headed back to Long Beach with George.

We all went to bed and my father would really wake me up having me to go downstairs to get him some soda every hour. That really made me very upset because I couldn't get enough sleep and while this was going on, the marriage of my parents was many tales.

When we all woke up the next morning, George took us to Cindy's house for breakfast before going to Disneyland. As we was eating our breakfast, she played a video about the late famous greatest gospel singer in the world Mahalia Jackson.

After we lefted Cindy's house, the five of us drove to Anahaim where Disneyland is located and going there made my day because my prayers were finally answered and we enjoyed ourselves while riding the rides at Disneyland. We was leaving Disneyland while the fireworks was flying in the air and it was in the evening.

We dropped Cindy home and the four of us headed back to George apartment in Long Beach so we can go to church Sunday. My daddy told me that we was driving back to

Richmond following services at church, so we was already packing our things. George decided to take us to Sunset Missionary Baptist Church on Sunday.

My cousin DeWayne was the pastor of Sunset and we had to drive back to Richmond following services because George told us that he had to go to work on Monday. After staying during the middle half of the service, we said goodbye to George and did our long drive back to Richmond once again through Central California.

I did indeed called my mother while I was spending the weekend with George and even though Disneyland was a memory that I will never forget, I missed my mother while I was gone and my father and I had our differences during the weekend vacation and after going to Disneyland for the first time, I wanted to go back.

After we arrived back in Richmond while the sun was going down, I was very glad to see my mother and I felt much better. I want to let everybody know that there is a very true saying and this saying is from the Wizard Of Oz movie that truly makes children feel better and it says "There is no place like home."

In September of 1991, I started my sixth grade year at Nystrom and it was my last year attending there because I was to walked away when I was graduating from there in June of 1992. My fifth grade teacher Douglas lefted Nystrom and he was a very generous man with a good heart and I missed him.

I thought that he was going to be my teacher again and he went to Oakland to teach at a school there. My new teacher was Donna Grove, who is a very close friend of mine and we still continue to keep in touched after I graduated. She was my teacher during my sixth grade year at Nystrom.

By the time that I went back to Nystrom, the whole school knew me and I knew them and I wasn't dealing with that many problems like I did when I start attending there in 1990 because we need to learn to face with certain things in life, even when we feel like giving up, but never give up because the Lord will blessed you and give you strength to overcome.

Before 1992 arrived to the scene, a man named Rodney King that was living in Los Angeles was in the news when some Los Angeles police officers beated him that became a another event. As they were talking about the story, it made history and made national news and it turned out to be the L.A. Riots in 1992.

The L.A. Riot became the second major riot in Los Angeles that occured since the famous 1965 Watts Riots, which occured during the Civil Rights Movement. Even though that 1992 was a upcoming new year, the marriage was still many tales that was ending.

The events that was going on in 1992 was the death of the famous bestselling African American author Alex Haley (who became famous by writing the bestselling book "Roots" and became a movie during the 1970's), Michael Jackson's "Dangerous" World Tour, the famous Olympics Games and the Presidental Election.

President Bush was seeking a second four year term until leaving office in 1996, but there were two other candidates named Governor Bill Clinton and Ross Perot that were seeking the seat of federal leadership as President of the United States. Bill Clinton became involved with the Democratic Party and he won the 1992 Democratic Party.

Before Bill Clinton ran for president, he was Arkansas leader as governor and the third candidate Ross Perot was a Texas millionaire that was with the Independent Party. Even though 1992 really made history, the tales of my parents marriage was getting worser that it was like a person dying from AIDS and cancer.

The reason why that I said that is because when a person becomes real sick from a disease and when the disease keeps on developing inside of their body, then they died from it. The person infected from the disease can no longer deal with the consequences because the disease did it's job.

That's what I am talking about regarding the tales of the marriage of my parents and since the consequences was tales and the family love wasn't getting better, it was getting infected with a series of tales. My father and I was not getting along at all.

Everytime that my father and I was arguing, he was doing things such as getting mad at me, getting mad at me when I would defend my mother if he tell lies about her and used bad english towards me that made me upset and crying. If I would tell him that using bad english towards me was wrong, then he would denied it.

My father was a diabetic and he was blind. I learned much later on in my life that he was having moodswings. Moodswings involves with a person having personality changes and they will be "sweet and kind" one time and they will be upset at a another time.

I was really going through with my father and even though daddy was doing things that wasn't right, I still loved him and prayed for him day and night. I was really caught up between and I still was in the middle of my parents marriage. I truly hope and truly believe that somebody in the United States and around the entire world will understand this message.

While the many tales of my parents marriage was going on, there was a lot of people praying for the marriage to be saved because it should've been a everlasting marriage, but my mother's vision was different. She was praying to get out of the marriage, which made things go on worser.

In June of 1992, I went to the auditorium at Nystrom Elementary School because I was graduating. I was one of the class speakers at the graduation and the Lord gave me a speech. I wrote a short speech called "My Farewell To Nystrom" and the audience received a blessing from it.

I received something at the graduation that I never experience before in my life, which was a stand ovation from the principal, teachers, the Class of 1992, and the rest of the audience. Many days were coming by as the graduation was coming up and believe me, I was very nervous.

I wasn't expecting the stand ovation and to tell you the truth, I wasn't expecting the Lord to used me to preached at the event because God knew what he was doing and the Holy Ghost was using me that day. This is a memory that I will never forget and this event will always be in my heart forever.

I finally graduated elementary school and I was going to start a middle school in September of 1992. In July of 1992, I lefted out of town once again with my father and Arnold. Arnold became the driver of the blue Lincoln Town Car and we took a long trip to Greenwood, Louisiana for my family reunion.

The Birdsong family reunion was called the Ed and Ida Birdsong Family Reunion, who were my great grandparents (but passed away many years ago). We drove in the same direction like my parents and I along with my uncle Roosevelt did in 1986 when Jim passed away. We finally arrived in Greenwood around the afternoon.

We didn't stopped at any resting places while on the long road trip, but we stopped at one in Texas and my father was graceful to be back in his hometown. He wanted to go see one of his very close cousins and it was Henry and his wife Dorothy. She attend school with my father and she was very close to my father.

I met my other cousins, who were the children and grandchildren of Henry and Dorothy. I was telling them about the fun and sunny life in California. My father and I was staying for the Birdsong family reunion for a week and later on in the day, Arnold wanted to see his daughter somewhere else in Louisiana.

While Arnold went to go see his daughter, I was outside playing and talking to my cousins during our visit and one of my daddy's other cousins wanted us to stayed with him while we was visiting. It was my cousin Lewell and I called my mother in Richmond while visiting my relatives.

The family reunion was going on at a restaurant and the weather was very hot. Louisiana is very hot and since hot heat is really not my type of weather, I was running in and out of the building. I saw family members that I already know and I saw family members that I finally met for the first time.

About two days after my family reunion, my father and I finally went back home. Arnold came back with the car and we drove again for about two days. While we was visiting my relatives, my daddy and I wasn't getting along and I was ready to go home.

After taking the long road trip, we finally arrived in Richmond and I missed my mother while I was gone. The tales of my parents marriage was getting worser everyday and there wasn't no healing process coming on in to make the family love good like it should be when I was a little boy.

My father and I wasn't still getting along while we was away visiting our relatives in Greenwood and the many tales didn't stop growing between my mother and father. I started my first year of middle school at Adams Middle School in Richmond when September of 1992 arrived.

While I was attending Adams, I was going through a situation that really hurted my mother and a situation that affected me very much even though that I was innocent and caught up right in the middle of my parents marriage. It was in Satan's doing that cause this to happen.

I stopped preaching God's truthful message, I stopped reading my bible, I stopped playing my Gospel music, and not attending church that often. I was doing the Michael Jackson dance while all of the tales was going on and I would do Michael's popular moonwalk and his other movements.

The children at Adams would called me Michael everyday while we all was in school and it wasn't my fault. It was very bad that I was bringing home bad grades because of the many tales and the Michael Jackson dance. My mother knew that I received a calling on my life from the Lord nine years.

She knew that the Lord called me when I was only three years old after receiving the Holy Ghost and my father also knew it for himself. NASA made history when a astronaut named Dr. Mae Jemison became the very first African American woman in black history to fly into outer space.

Chapter Seven
A Family Love Breaking Up

In 1983, NASA made history when astronaut Dr. Sally Ride became the first American woman to ride in the space shuttle into outer space. I was blessed with a brand new bicycle that was my second bicycle on Christmas day of 1992. This bicycle had more features than my last bicycle and this new bicycle was a ten speed.

The spacecraft Galileo made a another flyby of the earth during December 8th, 1992 along with the moon and it was the spacecraft second flyby of the earth. The girls really admired me and liked me while I was at Adams and it followed me after leaving Nystrom in the graduation ceremony.

Some of the boys were teasing me at Adams and they were jealous of me because people were saying that James had all of the girls and I already mentioned that I wasn't expecting that to approach my way. I started to ride the Laidlaw school bus to school while I was attending Adams and I was still in special education.

I was also riding the public bus to school sometimes and things that were going on between my parents wasn't coming to a healing process, it was coming to a down fall and I was still a innocent victim of confusion. 1993 was a another year that was historical speaking and made major headlines.

President Bush lost to Governor Clinton in the 1992 Presidential Election and Bill Clinton became our new forty second President of the United States on January 20th, 1993, the New York bombing of the World Trade Center and the death of Arthur Ashe, a famous African American tennis player that died of AIDS.

Some of the other events that occured in 1993 was a religious cult that was going on in Waco, Texas and a man named Thurgood Marshall that became the very first African American to become United States Supreme Court justice in 1967 by the appointment of the late United States President Lyndon Johnson died.

Thurgood Marshall served on the Supreme Court from 1967 until he retired in 1991 and whatever a person is appointed for this job is serving for a lifetime. Even though I was about to come in contact to be thirteen years old on May 16th, the tales was still getting worser and worser between my parents.

I was still going through many things such as my grades while I was attending Adams was bad, praying and asking the Lord all the time to take me away and wanting to give up everyday while the tales was going on because I was getting tired of the many things not getting good like they were many years ago.

Before my thirteenth birthday arrived, I was coming home from school and after I walked inside, I saw my father lying on the kitchen floor as I was walking in the kitchen. His blood sugar rised up once again and he couldn't walked because he couldn't stand up straight and he was passing out.

He told me to walked him upstairs to his room and he couldn't hardly walked as I was helping him to his room. He went to his room and he was lying down in his bed and as he was lying down in his room, my mother returned home from school and after she came in, I told her about what happened to daddy.

My mother and I called the paramedics so they can take my father to Brookside Hospital. After they placed my father in a ambulance while taking him to the hospital, mama had her own key set during that time and we drove the car to the hospital.

My parents had their own set of keys during the time of marriage and when my mother drove the car to the hospital, she was driving it for the very first time in a longtime because my father didn't want my mother to use the car while the marriage was many tales.

After we arrived at the hospital, we had to go sit in the family waiting room and after we was sitting for awhile, a nurse finally called us in to go see my father. He was very happy after walking in to go visit him and we went back to the house after the doctor waited on him.

I stayed home by my mother's request the very next day regarding me taking care of my father. He appeared in the newspaper serving West Contra Costa County and it was the West County Times because he was going to be interview him while he was attending a Oakland A's baseball game.

It became his first major league baseball game and I was feeling upset because my father didn't take me to the game. Daddy decided to take one of his longtime friends to the game. This also hurted my mother that my father didn't take me to the game like a father that is for real takes his son to the game. My father two tickets to the game was free from the newspaper and while being interview at the game, he wanted to know if I wanted a gift from the game.

I decided for him to bring me back either a cap or a autograph baseball. When the tales of my parents marriage was having many downfalls, my mother would give me between twenty five to forty dollar allowances every month and my father would give me money too, but only one dollar.

My mother was giving me more than my father and when his story reached the public, he was doing two different stories. He told me that he was going to tell the newspaper that he was a father that had a son, but he didn't. His two stories were focus about sports mostly and the others were focus on his childhood, going around helping the people on welfare and being a minister.

He requested some copies of the newspaper because he was going to mailed them to our relatives. My prayers were answered after praying to experience this very special part of my life to live to see thirteen years old. I was a teenager and my parents knew that I wanted a another birthday party at home.

My thirteenth birthday was actually on a Sunday, but I decided to have my birthday party on Saturday, May 15th. I invited some of my friends to my small birthday party, including my neighbor Rochelle and my longtime friend Ian. Rochelle came to the party to help out by serving the guests.

My father was very upset at my mother because she wasn't there at the party and he was thinking that she should've been during that very special time in my life as a teenager. She was unable to come to the party because she had classes on that day.

After I started middle school in September of 1992, my mother decided to go back to school at Contra Costa College to become a nurse in private home care work and she wanted to learn more about the whole depth of the medical field. There are more and more people in the United States that are working in the field of medicine, law, and computer technology.

I did received a few birthday presents from my family members and friends and even though that I was happy as I was thirteen, I was still going through a lot. I was going through being the victim of confusion in my parents marriage, my father wouldn't want to change and him and I was still arguing, I was bringing home bad grades and dancing like Michael Jackson everyday.

My father and I was attending services every Sunday with Clim and JoEvelyn at Holy Mission Christian Center and while we was members at Holy Mission, my mother became a member at a church in Richmond called Gloryland Apostolic Cathedral later on. The pastor of this church was Bishop Tom Watson.

My father was still one of the ministers at Holy Mission when we became members in 1991 as it was getting started and during that time, my father was still preaching when his days was for him and he was still sitting in the pulpit. A popular chemical plant in Richmond released a cloud that made headlines in July of 1993. Denise was providing for my father during the morning at the house and as we was talking, a tank car that was at the chemical plant caught on fire.

The fire from the tank car created a big toxic cloud that went into San Pablo, Pinole, Hercules and headed towards the capitol of the State of California Sacramento. This cloud from the tank car made a lot of people sick and a few people died from it.

My mother was at school and she rushed home right after Contra Costa College found out about it because some of the fumes from the cloud traveled into her class and it made her sick. Several people and more in Richmond and close by towns had to be rushed to the hospital and there were helicopters flying and newsmedia rushing to the story.

There were many emergency officials driving over to the houses of the citizens that became sick and they were moving very fast to the chemical plant. This was a area wide emergency situation for the citizens of Richmond and nearby cities. It was becoming a travel eastward along San Pablo Bay and out laying areas that were around the bay.

The chemical plant was not too close to our house and we lived not too far from the Port of Richmond and the Santa Fe Richmond Train Yard, the Richmond Marina, and a oil refinery. While many people were getting medical attention after getting sick, daddy and I went to Kaiser Hospital in Richmond along with Denise.

When we arrived there, the newsmedia was doing interviews with several people and we was in a very long line of the many dozen of people that was sick. There were small rooms at the hospital that were like small clinics.

The building at the old Harry Ells High School was converted into a clinic regarding the chemical spill. There were people that were pouring all over Richmond and the nearby communities that had to receive medical attention and the building caught a lot of people attention because it was the major clinic.

The doctors and nurses at Harry Ells were out working on the field from Brookside Hospital. Perhaps the most bestknown and finest doctor in Richmond named Dr. Julius Robinson was there at Harry Ells supervising the other doctors and nurses during the time that people were coming for medical attention.

He was working at Brookside during that time and he was also my parents doctor when I was a baby. I went back to school in September of 1993 to start my eighth grade year at Adams that became my graduating year because I was finally getting ready to start my freshman year in high school.

I was slowing down with the Michael Jackson dance because in my mind, I already knew that the Lord was going to bring this situation to pass soon, but I had to wait and I prayed during the many tales everyday until it ended.

On October 19th, 1993, I was walking to the bus stop when my dog Tony ran to the other side of the fence. He was always doing that everytime that I went to the bus stop. After Adams let out for the day, I went to the backyard to see Tony while checking on him and he was gone. Tony attacked my father when he was putting his shoe brushes on the backyard porch.

Chapter Eight
Approaching A Separation

He was washing them in the laundry room before Tony attacked him. He had to received some medical attention from Brookside Hospital. The doctor at Brookside Hospital told daddy that he should call to the Contra Costa County animal services so the officer can make a report.

My father didn't like Tony and he knew then that the dog was going to attacked him and during the period of the many tales, we was still having problems with Tony. The officer came over and she told us that Tony needed to be away from the backyard, so we kept him in the downstairs bathroom for ten days.

We let Tony back in the backyard and I was upset at him when this happen. Tony wasn't in the backyard on October 19th when I came home from school. My father was at home after I lefted to go to school and when my mother lefted to go to school.

I was wondering where Tony was at and Tony placed a big hole in the backyard fence, but Tony was unable to attempt to make his way out because he was a large dog. We never saw him ever again and I will never forget him because he was my first dog and I had him for five years.

I always wanted a dog and it lefted my heart broken into the many pieces of a puzzle and to tell you the truth, I asked myself "Why this is happening to me and why my father was doing this to his wife and son?" But it was the part of the devil's plan and that came to my mind much later. It is like a remind thinking of a person that is lying down dying.

The reason why that I said that because it will put a affect on the people that love and care for them and that brought me a reminder about my dog. I still missed him today and it gave me a broken heart when he was no longer around because he was a blessing to me from the Lord.

I still think about him all the time and I really don't know if he is still living or not, but the everlasting memories of him will always remain in my heart and nothing cannot take it out of my heart and as long this book and the message of hope is being heard worldwide, it will encourage a person.

In December of 1993, I was attending therapy and while I was in therapy, people were still praying and asking the Lord for the marriage to be save, but my mother was praying to get out of the marriage. I would tell my parents to stop arguing when I would try to focus on certain things and that was including my homework assignments.

When the verbal abuse had a affect on me when my parents was arguing, my mother felt my pain and my father didn't care. He would either tell his side of the story that my mother caused it or he would tell me to stay out of the arguments and daddy was the one that would cause the arguments.

He would get on my mother about certain things and that made me a victim of confusion. My father also brought something to my way that placed a stressful upsetting load on my back when the marriage became many tales.

Before the Christmas season of 1993, I called my cousin Willis in Greenwood asking for some money so I can go purchase a train set. My father brought my first two train sets for Christmas when I was seven and eight years old. They both were gifts from my parents.

Before I called my cousin, my father told me a few days before to don't asked Willis for any money. He would asked the members of our family for some money, but it wasn't okay for me. Willis did mailed me a check and he also mailed me a second check from our cousin Lewell along with his.

My mother called Willis after the checks arrived in the mail after she asked for his phone number regarding the checks. She called Willis on her own phone and she received her own telephone line in 1991 because my father was rushing her off the phone. During that time of the many tales, he was also listening to her phone conversations and he was also doing the same thing to me.

He was listening to my conversations when I would talk to many friends and classmates and he would embarrased me when he would tell me to hurry up and get off the phone so he could make some phone calls and not only he was controlling the phone, but daddy was controlling everything during the many tales.

My mother told me that I didn't do anything wrong while asking Willis for the money. My mother and I then took a city bus over to Hilltop Mall in Richmond and we went to a very popular store called Kay Bee toy store.

The last two years of this book is going to be the main story because 1994 and 1995 had many events that made history around the world and the tales of my parents marriage was approaching a separation. It's so hard to talk about, but a person reading this book will hopefully understand.

I was still going through a lot and my father wasn't the same father that I knew so many years ago. He wasn't performing the task of a father like a real father does with his son and when I see these fathers spending time with their sons and teaching him things, I say to myself "I wish that daddy was doing those things with me".

He would tell me that he loved me very much, but he only gave me one dollar and he wasn't spending enough time with me while the many tales was going on and I want to let the many fathers of today know that if you have three hundred dollars and every bill was already paid for, then share with your sons.

My mother and I wanted to moved out of the house after things wasn't getting any better. A separation was approaching during the downfall of my parents marriage and since the Lord brought this my way as a message of hope, my mother was taking a stand of filing for a divorce.

That is something that no child don't ever want to experience because they want their parents to stay together and they want the family love to last a lifetime instead of being apart. Now that is something that some people don't want to take.

The reason why that I said that because a child is the innocent victim when it comes for the divorce of their parents and during the time that they are going through and they become very stress and sensitive to the abuse and other problems.

I was still attending therapy and my mother was getting support and her counseling from the Battered Women Program. I was trying to sleep during the many evenings, but I couldn't because during the downfall of my parents marriage cause me to have many causes of nightmares and crying a lot.

My father was still yelling at me and we was still having daily arguments a lot and I was still bringing home bad grades. Before I graduated Adams in June of 1994, Adams was having their yearly annual award ceremony and my special education teacher nominated me for my curriculum assistance class and I was her only student that was nominated for the award.

My teacher that nominated me was a woman named Bonnie and after my mother found out about it, she was very proud of me and daddy also knew about it. I wasn't to take home that award and I still have the award today. My father wanted to go to the Adams Middle School award ceremony, but I didn't wanted him to be there.

I didn't wanted my father to be there because of the many times that he embarrased me. The award ceremony was during the evening and I was blessed to take my award home and daddy told me before the award ceremony that he was going to asked one of his friends to take him to the ceremony in his car, but they never came.

I also received an award three years earlier in the fifth grade from my teacher for the Best Scholar in the whole class in 1991 during the Class of 1991 graduation at Nystrom right along with my Best Citizenship award. I also was the winner of the Science Fair award at Ellerhorst in my forth grade year in my class.

My mother and I rode the bus over to the annual award ceremony and Bonnie gave us a ride home after it was over. I was blessed to have the award and it will become something that I will keep as a treasure for life. In June of 1994, I completed Adams from graduating and it was a blessing that I was going to the higher level of high school and I was still going through.

I didn't attend the Class of 1994 ceremony because I was going through a lot at Adams and it wasn't meant for me to be present at the graduation ceremony. My english teacher gave me my award certificate of graduation the very next day at school. The many students that graduated in my class was given a party.

Speaking on the graduation party, my mother brought me a brand new white tuxedo for the graduation party at the gym and people were given me a lot of compliments and I received the most from the girls at Adams that admired me and respected me. There were some people at Adams that nominated me for the prettiest eyes.

This was going on before I graduated Adams and I didn't become a winner, but I wasn't expecting the girls to give me a vote while we was getting ready to graduate for a boy that had eyes that were the prettiest eyes for the yearbook.

I had to go to DeAnza High School in El Sobrante for not passing a math part of a State of California test. I was attending summer school at DeAnza for six weeks and it was just only the beginning of the high school life. Richmond lost it's most respected doctor on June 25th, 1994 and it was Dr. Julius Robinson. He was dealing with a battle of lung cancer that he was battling with every since 1989.

He was truly a great doctor, role model and he was truly a leader that was a leader, not a follower. My parents and a lot of people all over Richmond and other places went to see visited him before he died at Brookside Hospital in San Pablo. He was a true edition to Richmond and mostly the African American community.

Girls were approaching my way as I was at DeAnza High for summer school and some of the boys were very jealous of me and it became a following process starting out of Nystrom. Things were becoming worser while my parents was married and a separation was becoming a building process and it was a downfall.

I finally started high school in September of 1994 as a freshman at John F. Kennedy High School in Richmond. I wasn't happy during the time that I started Kennedy because I didn't wanted to attend the school and it wasn't my type. I was very happy when I started ninth grade, but I wanted to leave the school and Kennedy brought me back memories when I was attending Nystrom a few weeks earlier and it is a all black high school. It wasn't the Kennedy building that it was causing the problem, it was some of the students.

Chapter Nine
Into The Separation

I was still dealing with many temperations and trials and during the many tales of my parents marriage, it was coming to a closing of a book very slowly and being a teenager at the age of fourteen years old was very difficult for me during that time. The special family love that was placed together by God was no longer special like it was many years ago.

My mother had to withdraw from all of her classes that involves with the medical field because she had a knee injury. My parents were in and out of court and while I was still caught up between the middle of their marriage, the judge gave my mother something that is still occurs today and it was a restraining order.

This order was for her protection and she was in Pinole getting a treatment for her left arm and while she suffered from walking and riding the bus, she had a lump on her left arm. This problem was caused by being out in the cold weather and carrying grocery bags that were very heavy.

My mother joined a church in Richmond in 1994 called the Church of Deliverance and it is very close to the church that my father and I was attending and it was Holy Mission. A man named Apostle Saint Samuel Vann pastors the Church of Deliverance in Richmond and my mother was part of their church administration.

While she was on her way to mailed some papers for the business matters for the Church of Deliverance, she was going to Berkeley on the bus and she was running to catch it. After she was trying to catch the bus, she fell into a large hole.

The hole was located in a street next to a sidewalk and a man took my mother to a bench before the paramedics came and there were many times that I saw my mother walking when I would ride in the car with my father to go places with him.

While the many tales was becoming a separation, the Lord gave me something to do that was placed on my heart and it was this book. I was thinking about the many people worldwide that need a message of hope of miracles and a encouraging message of God in a truthful message.

My mother told me that she was also going to write her a book about her experiences in order to help others. She never wrote one and I will hope that she will one of these days. My mother is a very strong American Indian mixed woman who goes by faith and she supported me and the message of hope of this book.

It was two weeks before Christmas in December of 1994 and two weeks did went by fast. My mother came home during the evening and I was getting worried. She told me to look out of a window and what my mother brought home really shocked me.

She pulled up a grey 1994 Ford Tempo GL Sedan in the driveway and it was the Lord's blessing for her. Her days of riding the bus and walking were finally over because she already suffered from the affects of the cold weather and coming home with very heavy bags of groceries and getting rides from her friends and members of her church. She already went through for about five to six years of not having a car.

My Christmas on December 25th, 1994 along with my parents became the very last Christmas that we spent together. There was several times that I would wonder when my mother and I are going to packed up and moved out of the house. I want to tell all of the children and teenagers in every nation around the world today the meanings of these facts in not a drama play.

1995 is the last year of this book because it covers the closing of the marriage and the many tales. After many years of wondering and praying, the separation was closing up very quickly. Children that experience these stages over the years and after God blesses them, it will make them strong and that goes for everybody.

Before my mother and I moved out of the house, I already packed some of my things before 1994 ended. While I was still attending Kennedy High School, the judge issued a statement that we should moved out of the house at a certain time. This kind of situation really affects the child the most because the family love broken up.

I am pretty sure that you all want to know what the word family love means, then I will tell you. Family love is that familyship with love that only God can give, not man. A family is a spiritual blessing from the Lord and if they help one another during times of tests and trials, then that love will last forever and strive to last forever. If that family is about to become apart because of specific reasons, then the family love won't unite as a whole family because it is many pieces of a broken glass vase.

Before my mother and I moved out of the house, she was looking around for some houses in a much nicer neighborhood. She looked in El Cerrito and Berkeley for a little while. Those two places wasn't in the Lord's will. We was still getting boxes to packed up our things.

A pastor in Richmond that knew my mother named Fredrick wanted my mother and I to moved in with him and his family. The ending of this marriage was like a book closing and people knew within themselves that it was time for my mother to move on and little James was innocent.

My mother was going to stay with Fredrick and his family until we can get our own place. He knew about the situation regarding my mother not being treated right and I was still in the middle of the many tales. I was still wishing that things were getting better like it was when I was a little boy.

On March 27th, 1995, I was at church and I told everybody that my mother and I was moving out of the house because the fifteen year marriage of my parents was ending through a divorce. Daddy wasn't there during the services and I told them that the "good memories" will always remain in my heart.

I asked Clim to watched out for my father while I was not able to be with him and he said that he would. Before my grandmother Charlene died, she asked Clim to watched out for daddy and Clim also told her that he would. On March 28th, 1995, I stayed home from school because my mother and I was moving.

My parents were no longer married and my mother had Fredrick and two of his friends to load many things in the back of our car and in Fredrick's car plus in the back of a truck. It all came to pass because the family love was no longer a together glass vase, it was a broken glass vase.

We wanted to take two things, which was a oak server and the piano that my father brought me. The oak server matched a oak dining room set that we had and the attorney that was working with my mother didn't write down that the server was included furniture of the dining room set.

The Richmond Police Department was called over regarding the piano and the server. We couldn't take both belongings and my father kept the piano and the server and the majority of many belongings that was my mother and myself was taken to a building at the Ark of Jesus Holiness Church in Richmond.

The building at this church is a storage building and Bishop Arthur Eames is the pastor of this church. He already knew my mother for a longtime and later on during March 28th, we were no longer living at Maine Avenue and my parents were divorced. Even though that the ending of the marriage of my parents was over, this book don't stop talking to all nations.

This message of hope must go on and my mother and I moved in with Fredrick and his family. We would attend church services together and my mother told me that we was living there until we can get our own place of residence.

The judge at the Contra Costa Courthouse in Martinez, California issued visitation rights to go visit my father and I was visiting and calling my father during the time that my mother and I lefted to go live with Fredrick and his family. As my mother was looking around for a place to live, a different city was in mind.

The Lord placed it on my mother's heart to go searched in Solano County in the county seat city of Fairfield, California. I didn't find out about this until my mother told me and we wasn't staying with them for a longtime because we was put out by them.

There are two scriptures from the bible that talks about leaders that are leaders of the Gospel. This consists of pastors, leaders of the church and preachers that are going by the right standards of the rules like a child sometimes don't go by some rules during school.

"Yea, they are greedy dogs which can never have enough, and they are shepherds that cannot understand: they look to their own way, every one for his gain, from his quarter. "
Isaiah 56:11

"Therefore thus saith the Lord God of Israel against the pastors that feed my people; Ye had scattered my flock, and driven them away, and have not visited them: behold, I will visit upon you the evil of your doings, saith the Lord."
Jeremiah 23:2

We was lefted homeless and we start staying at the men's center of the Church of Deliverance that was next to the church. Pastor Vann heard about the news and he decided to give us a room while we was getting ready to live in Fairfield.

My mother and I was sharing the same room and some of the men that were members of the Church of Deliverance had to go sleep upstairs so the downstairs area was occupied for my mother and I and Pastor Vann would stop by the men's center daily to come and see if things were all well.

The kitchen of the men's center was upstairs and in order for us to use it, my mother would have me to go upstairs to double check if it was alright for us to use. I told my father during a visit that my mother and I was moving to Fairfield and after I told him, he was very shocked to hear the news.

I also told my friends and classmates in the neighborhood and Kennedy High that I was moving to Fairfield and they were very shocked to hear that because they didn't want me to leave, but my mother and I already been through a lot over the years. The good memories of the early days will remain in my heart.

While I was at Kennedy High, the only thing that I prayed for is to leave the school to go attend a school that settled firm in a nicer environment that I can deal with. I was having some good times at Kennedy, but I felt like that I should've lefted from the first time that I started attending there.

My mother and I stayed at the men's center until June of 1995 because we was getting ready to move to Fairfield. Our prayers were finally answered when we moved out of Richmond to go live in Fairfield on June 14th, 1995. It reminded me of the special land that was called the Promised Land from the Lord.

The whole concept in Fairfield was very different from Richmond and the concept is very peaceful and quiet, the learning process of education is very interesting and pleasing and the many people are very friendly and helpful. While we were living in Fairfield, I continue to visit and spend some weekends with him.

My father was missing pieces of a pie that was taken out, which was his ex wife and son. There were a lot of times that I indeed asked my father if he misses his ex wife instead of me and daddy would say "Do she missed me?" He would tell people that he loved me and misses me, but my mother was lefted out and he did missed my mother.

I was getting ready to attend a new school in a different place with a different atmosphere during my sophomore year. When August of 1995 arrived, I stopped visiting my father in Richmond during three months because God finally brought me back in the ministry and the Lord was preparing me for my first sermon.

The Lord was preparing me for my first sermon and while working on it, I was still mad at my father for doing "repeatable things" like the many tales that was going on between my parents. Around the time that I stopped visiting my father, I was praying during that time because I was hoping that daddy would understand me.

In September of 1995, I started my tenth grade year at my whole new school and I already mentioned that the school was Fairfield High School. My mother and I went back to Kennedy High regarding my transcripts and they finally gave them to me.

Chapter Ten
Lord, We Are No Longer Together As A Family

I start attending Fairfield High School on September 7th, 1995 after getting my transcripts from Kennedy High. This new school was different from my last high school. The whole concept about my last school couldn't compare to this school because it truly made me belong to Fairfield High.

The teachers and students at Fairfield High were very friendly and very sweet and kind. Since the Lord was using me to witness the Word of God to the people at the school, I wasn't expecting the students to go home and telling the members of their family (including their parents) about me. Their parents and relatives wanted to meet me and I already met many of them.

I became a very popular person at Fairfield High School during the time that I was a new at the school and the girls respected me, liked me and admired me very much. My mother and I attended church services at the New Beginnings Spiritual Hospital, which was located in Fairfield.

The New Beginnings Spiritual Hospital wasn't a church building, it was under the New Beginnings Ministry of Love church located in Santa Rosa, California. The Spiritual Hospital had a program that was designed to help people that were using drugs and they were living at the Spiritual Hospital.

The program was helping the residents to give their lives over to Jesus Christ and helping them to graduate out of the program. My mother learned about the Spiritual Hospital after the pastor of the Santa Rosa church told her about it a while back.

A woman named Claudia was the pastor of New Beginnings Spiritual Hospital and the pastor of New Beginnings Ministry of Love Church is Pastor Cecil Hale, Jr. He was the overseer pastor of Fairfield New Beginnings and he is the overseer pastor of the Merced church and the San Bernardino, California New Beginnings.

Him and his wife Sister Anita Hale already knew my mother before the separation came and while we was helping around and attending church services every Friday night at New Beginnings of Fairfield and visiting the residents everyday. The Lord was still preparing me to preached my first sermon in December of 1995.

When I called my father every week, he was asking me over eleven times when I was coming back to visit him. I was going to visited my father again and I was waiting on the Lord. I made a telephone call to Clim in November of 1995 and I told him that I was coming home to see my father after three months.

I also told him that the Lord was having me to preached a sermon that was my very first one and he told me that I can come forward to preached it on and I told him later on to don't tell my father that I was coming to visit him for the weekend. My mother already knew about it and she told me that daddy was going to be uplifted with joy and be very happy to see me after three months.

The sermon that the Lord gave me was for my father and I was finally on my way to see him and it was on December 1st, 1995 when school was over with for the day and I told my father about a few months that I was coming back home to see him, but I didn't say when.

I was feeling very nervous as my mother and I was on the freeway as we was on our way to my father's house in Richmond. She waited for me outside while I was getting ready to make a grand entrance by surprising him and I already knew that we was about to reunite after I stopped visiting him for three months.

My father heard the doorbell rang as I was ringing it and during the time that I was ringing it, one of his tenants came to answer the door and I told her to say nothing as I was about to surprise him after three months. After she let me inside, my father really wanted to know who was at the door.

I was walking upstairs to his room very quietly and I was almost walking my half way, but my father howled out "Jr" when he walked downstairs finding out who rang the doorbell.

We hugged as father and son reunited after three months and he was very happy, lifted with joy and very glad to see me.

He knew that it was me and I went back outside to say a farewell to my mother for the weekend and she drove home. I told my father about how much the Lord have blessed me, the church that I became a part off and how much that I enjoyed my high school. He already knew that I was impress about Fairfield.

I told my father that I was visiting him because I was preaching my very first sermon on Sunday and he was shocked about it during the time that we was still talking. He knew that the Lord already saved me and called me to be a preacher by the time that I turned three years old.

On December 3rd, 1995, I finally went up to preached the message that the Lord placed on my heart to speak. Clim let me go forward before him and the church was Holy Mission. The sermon was coming from the Ephesians 6:4 and it deals with fathers and their duties for their children.

The message of Ephesians 6:4 say a very true meaning and today's fathers need to abide by this because it is his task to be honest and truthful to his family and that is from the Lord Jesus Christ and he wants every father to know about Ephesians 6:4. The honest message says...

"And ye fathers, provoke not your children to wrath, but bring them up in the training and admonition of the Lord."

That message was for my father and he was very upset. The honest truth was spoken and God was trying to tell him something. During these last days, I will pray and hope that the fathers nationwide will take a stand and be a positive rolemodel and a living example to their children.

I went back to the house after church was over. My mother called me and told me that she was on her way to picked me up. My father didn't have that much to say to me after church and after packing up my things, my mother and I lefted and headed to the Interstate 80 freeway to go home. I had to start school on Monday. I decided to called my father until the next week because he was mad during the service and I was letting things between him and I get better again and I was still praying for him everyday.

It was a message of fatherhood that the Lord gave me to preached at church and sometimes we may not take the certain things deeply in the truth and we may get upset about it because it have strong powerful words. We all must pray and asked God to guide footsteps so all of us can learned how to take the truth.

I truly thank the Lord for grace and mercy, his word and special family love with all families and this book have truly ministered to me a lot while working on it. I will keep the faith and having faith in God that this book will become a success to many millions worldwide.

After I turned seventeen years old on May 16th, my father passed away on June 10th, 1997 and I wasn't fighting him back or getting back at him in this book and he will never lived to see a message of hope (this book} or my future gospel albums be featured during award ceremonies and other important programs.

He would've been proud of me and if your father did many serious things to you that are not right and if you live with your mother when you are in her care, go visited your father sometimes during the times that you and him are feuding and this is also including him hurting your feelings and if he abused you.

The reason why that I said that because he will feel very lonely that he will feel very sorry of what he have done to his children and his wife and he will missed them very much and if you visited your father and encourage him and forgive him for the many things that he have done, then the Lord will forgive you.

Chapter Eleven
A Message Of Hope

I visited my father as much as I can even though I was unable to everyday and I called him every week. After he died, I came to one conclusion and that is I already forgave my father from everything that he done to me after I moved out of my hometown to live in Fairfield.

This is my message of hope of the conclusion of this book and I already mentioned that this book taught me many things about true life issues. This book taught me the many ways of manhood and to become a person that is not afraid to speak out in what I truly believe in and the things that represents truth.

My father didn't sit down with me somedays and teached me the one hundred percent things about manhood and all of the honest details about it. I did learned somethings from my father just before he died. The Lord and his guidence of this book already taught me about manhood and the steps of it already.

I thank God that I indeed called my father and traveling once a month or every now and then to visited him and this truthful message in this message of hope will help somebody in a nation around the world because this world truly needs a message that talks about hope.

This book also taught me about enjoying family life in a love called family love because starting or having a family becomes a blessing from the ordaining of God and if a family remembers to pray together, then they will stay together and the special family love will last forever.

This book also taught me about children because they are special and a blessing from God and the future of tomorrow. I must really say that children may get out of line sometimes, but never pushed them or drive them away because God gave you them.

This book will help millions and millions of people and children around the world and continue to help a another million worldwide because a true message of hope is spoken and we all need a honest message with the message of the Lord, love, harmony, peace within peace and good hope.

It is a blessing from the Lord to have a message of hope because the world needs it and throughout the years, you will hear people talking about it and many people receiving it into their everyday daily lives. Somebody in a country around the world should become thankful for it because it will carry their wings.

It will carry their wings in their walk in the Christian journey and childhood, military career, relationship with their companion and their education. That is very amazing about that and remember that the truth must be spoken and it must be heard always because a certain part of it will have a message of hope.

Before I close this conclusion, I want to thank God for allowing me to share my story, testimony, words, truth and the very honest message of hope in this book because it was his grace and amazing mercy that put this all together to share with many people around the world because it is the Word of God that is the whole concept of a message of hope and may the Lord be with you always.

Selected Messages From Very Special Friends

Dear James,

God bless you, I am so glad that you reserved me a page. Well, I'm glad that we are still friends and I hope that we will always. I hope that God will bless you forever, bless you with your book, and your future. We both should go on tour along with Shirley Caesar, Kirk Franklin, and Angelo & Veronica.

May God Bless You,
Fermin Maturin, Jr.
Fairfield High School

Brother James,

Stay sweet and kind, don't ever change. Satan is out to kill you, but stay in the Lord and keep me in your prayers as you pray everyday. I love you so much and you really blessed the world with the gift of God.

God Bless You,
Normaila Mills
Fairfield High School

Brother James,

Hi, it's me again. It's been a long year and by the grace of God, we made it through. I am very sorry to hear about your father, but a least we know that he's in a better place. James, I hope that you will continue to be sucessful in every thing you do. When times gets rough, don't let nobody tell you different from what God placed in you. Well James, I guess that I will talk to you later and stay truly blessed.

God Bless You,
Joshua Bone

To James,

Have a wonderful summer. I will pray that the Lord will bless you with a young woman who's heart is as big and beautiful as yours. Pray that God's will be done in my life. My heart goes out to you and your beautiful mother and may God bless the both of you.

I Love You Always,
Kim Ritchie
Fairfield High School

Dear James,

Hey once again, I want to thank you for being such a loyal friend to me. You walked around Fairfield High School with your pride, dignity, and face to the sky. I really just wanted to say that it feel good to be here with you knowing that you will be beside me all the time. You are very respected by me and I will never forget you and you are really a true inspiration. I believe that oneday, you'll suceed in your gospel singing and be rated at the top with Shirley Caesar and the rest of the great gospel singers. You'll really get what you really deserve and walk the golden streets of heaven and you are a true child of God.

Love You Lots,
Samantha Mills
Fairfield High School

Their messages placed me through in the many tests and trials of my life, even when my father died. These five people really let me know that I am a true Man of God and they also reminded me that James Birdsong, Jr. is a person and a human being with feelings like everybody else in the world.

The messages that Fermin, Kim, Normaila, Samantha, and Joshua wrote to me were a message from the Lord because these special friends were Godsent to me when other people turned away after I helped them, supported them, and most of all, opening family love to them. I will pray that these words will encourage many people to go after their dreams in life.

The other people that will tell you that you sing, write, and act are going to wish that they didn't tell you no because God finally elevated you to a higher authority than them and those people are going to become your friends and I am here to share this, only reached out to your true friends that love you.

Written Speeches By Evangelist James Birdsong, Jr.

Fathers, Share With Your Sons
A Speech Written By James Birdsong, Jr.

It is very important fathers that it is your job and your task to be a example to your sons and teaching him the step and ways of manhood. Fatherhood is a blessing to a boy and if God's pure grace and mercy didn't exist at all, then a boy growing up into a man will be lost as the children of Isreal were running forty years in the wilderness.

But I come before you in Jesus name to let every father around the world to know today that you should always share your money and anything else with your sons whatever you receive. It don't matter if you have three hundred dollars and your bills already paid, then divide it with your sons by giving him half of it.

That is your responsibility to share many things with your wife and children, especially your sons. A father that is very happy and blessed with a son should be happy and thankful and he have somebody to talk to and the son have a man to talk to and teach him how to be a man, a good husband to the special someone that will be his wife, and a good father to his children.

When the sons is a grown man and becomes very sucessful during his life, then he will help his father back in return. It don't matter if you have five hundred dollars and the bills were paid, then share it with your sons. It doesn't matter how much amount small or large it maybe, then share it with your sons.

Carrying My Faith To Survive
A Speech Written By James Birdsong, Jr.

In whatever I go through and in whatever I must face and battle through in my life, I will carry my faith to survive in whatever things are either good or bad because I am on my way to a better place and that is heaven. It will be a survival that will always dwell inside of my soul forever.

If I go through with my family and friends and they tell James that they don't love him anymore or they want him out of family love view, then he will carry his wings for survival and I know that God's grace and mercy still prevails.

I will carry my faith to survive in my life because God's pure grace and mercy still prevails inside of me. If things get from good to bad, then I will carry my faith to survive through good times and the bad times and through the storm and the rain.

Even though that I kept the faith in my dreams and goals while I was dreaming from the time that I was a young boy, faith also became a survival in my life and it kept me strong while things became bad and the Lord made the bad things passed away so they can be good again and I am a living witness to that.

I will carry the faith to help me survive the trials and many tests that I had to go through and what I already went through over the years. If you have the heart and courage to carry the faith to survive, then you should thank God for that and works of courage will help you survive.

Reaching To A Better Place
A Speech Written By James Birdsong, Jr.

I must say this message of truth on this very day because every man, woman, and child go through the many things in their family ship, friendship, and relationship with their relatives, friends, and companions. But we all are experience to the many bad things that are going on in our world.

You hear news reports about drive by shootings and the children are in the middle of the crossfire. You hear about world nations fighting against one another. You hear about children in ghettos in the major United States cities joining gangs and taking drugs and guns to school and using them to messed up their dreams.

You hear about innocent people getting killed, children getting killed and killing each other, racism building up more and leads sometimes to death, AIDS and other diseases taking many people's lives and many people are not going to church like they should.

I'm here to let the world know that these things will be passed away very soon because we are reaching to a better place because there will be joy, peace, harmony, and love and Jesus will stand right there with his children forever and forever in peace.

This place is the promised land in which the late Martin Luther King, Jr. said a longtime of ago before his death. Heaven awaits for us and heaven is the better place that we are going to stand up one day and picked up our wings bounded for the next airport.

I Can Do All Things Through Christ Which Strengtheneth Me
A Speech Written By James Birdsong, Jr.

In Philippians 4:13, it have a very true message in it which a lot of people nowdays don't want to abide by and as long we have a dream in life, we can say "I can do all things through Christ which strengthenth me" and that is the very truth from Philippians 4:13.

A lot of people and mostly our children have dreams and some goal in life and as long you have the Lord standing along the way to guide your footsteps to accomplish your dream. I don't care what the devil or any man is saying, you are going to be a somebody in your life.

While you are fighting the many things to accomplish a dream, there are going to be some people and your relatives that are going to say that you are not going to make it, they will say that you are not going to last long, and they will really put you down from going after your dream.

If they do this to you my brothers and sisters, you must let them know that you are going to make it with God by your side and I know that my dream is going to come true because I know that I can do all things through Christ which strengthenth me because I am going to be a somebody no matter what people say or think.

Always Love Your Children
A Speech Written By James Birdsong, Jr.

All of us should love our children because they are the most precious blessing that any man or woman can ever have. I know that our children can do things that don't look right or some thing kind of strange, but always love them no matter how bad or good they are and that is what God wants the adults to do.

If you don't love them, then you are really hurting yourself more than you are hurting their feelings. Something is really going on with some parents not loving their children or don't care for them that I just don't understand. In the Bible, the Lord Jesus said "Suffer little children, and forbid them not, to come unto me, for of such a kingdom of heaven".

Now that is very true because it does have a lot to do about our children hurting, crying, want their parents to love them, and being abused. We should love our children because God put them into our lives and they will become very sucessful while they learned.

Always love them and if they need somebody to talk to, go on ahead and talk to them. If they need prayer, then go on ahead and pray with them. It doesn't matter what the situation will be, always love them because later in life, the children will say a lot of good things about you when they reached the next stage of life, which is adulthood. Remember that the children is the prescious gift of all and they are our children.

The Grandmother Is The Mother Of All Mothers
A Speech Written By James Birdsong, Jr.

Even though my grandmother Charlene and Mildred are no longer around, I learned a lot about them and I was blessed with them even though they never lived to see me grow up. I really thank God for grandmothers because not only she really cares for her grandchildren, but she is the mother of all mothers.

When mothers don't want their children no more and if mothers don't love their children no more, then the grandmother really steps on in and opened up her arms out to them and follows the rules of family love because she have a very special love that nobody can't touched.

She is the shepherd, example of motherhood, inspiration, stand strong for mothers, and positive rolemodel for mothers because she is the mother of all mothers and she already headed a ship for mothers and sailing across the waters of motherhood. Today my brothers and sisters, we should say thank you Jesus for the grandmothers in our lives.

America Needs To Listen Now
A Speech Written By James Birdsong, Jr.

The Lord have really blessed our country and since we are living in the last days now, a lot of Americans are not going by several rules of living and a lot of Americans are not living by a simple word called the Word of God. Our country are getting more exposed to violence in schools, gang violence, violence in our communities and to our children and drugs and diseases are rising up more.

There are many other, things that are going on in America because times are getting worser now than before. The things that occured in the United States a few decades ago such as the certain prices of items are higher than they were back then and the many records in health care ins not the same like as it was many years ago.

I truly pray for the United States because this land that became a land of liberty needs the Lord and listen to the ways of "truth and self liberty" by listening now to the ways of God's strongful word. Several times over several times that many Americans losing their lives to drugs and violence and I truly believe that people of America will be healed if they start listening now.

He Lefted So Soon Lord
A Tribute To The Late James Charles Birdsong, Sr.
Written By James Birdsong, Jr.

This is a tribute to the memory of my father Mr. James Charles Birdsong, Sr., who passed away on June 10th, 1997 as the summer was arriving and one month before his birthday. Daddy was going to be fifty nine years old on July 19th and since this truthful message of hope includes seven speeches that I have wrote, this one makes eight all together.

I know that my father and I had our hard times while my mother was married to my father, but I do have many good memories that I can remember spending with my father and they were only those memories of the good times growing up as a young boy. A another memory of my father were the times that we were very close many times while I was a baby.

My father was the one that brought my school clothes everytime that September arrived and he was the one that brought my gifts for Christmas when I was a young boy. I will never forget daddy and as long as I live, daddy will always remain very close into my heart. This would've made him very happy and proud.

I will also never forget the time when decided to take me into Anahaim, California where Disneyland is located. I really asked my parents and pray to go to Disneyland and when my father took me down there, I was eleven years old and we went to Disneyland as we was visiting our cousin George in Long Beach. After daddy and I went to Disneyland, we would talk about it a lot.

Daddy taught me a lot about our family, which is the Birdsong family roots. Not only our family roots, but our heritage, our generation, and our church background, which is a Baptist back ground. Everything that he taught me about our family and it's heritage will be something that I will passed down to his next generation, which is my future children.

I will passed it on down to my future children along with the other family background that I have and it's my mother's. Some of the gospel songs that I heard Patti LaBelle sing on special award ceremonies, she would say "Pass it on" and her song "When You Been Blessed (Feels Like Heaven)" mentioned that.

He will never live to see me get married to that very special someone and he will never live to meet his grandchildren. Just before he died, I mailed him his Father's Day card before this day called Father's Day was coming up. He told me that he will always cherished it and he died a few days before Father's Day and I was going to visited him for Father's Day.

I know that he would've said "Son, you must move on with your life and always move on with your career". He lefted very soon and daddy would've been very happy that his only child finally made it through the storm as a lot of people in the church talk about a very midst of a storm that they went through. I indeed made it through the storm and that is my testimony.

Index

Africa
- South Africa

Airlines
- Delta
- TWA

Airports
- Dallas/Ft. Worth
- Los Angeles
- San Francisco
- Shreveport

Ashe
- Arthur

Astronauts
- Jemison, Mae J.,
- McAuliffe, Sharon
- Ride, Sally K.,

BART
- Transbay Tube
- West Oakland Station

Birdsong
- Charlene
- Ed, Jr.,
- Ed, Sr.,
- Ida
- Jim
- Mary
- Robert James

- Ruby

Bombing
- World Trade Center

Bridge
- Bay Bridge

Bus Lines
- Greyhound
- Laidlaw
- Trailways

California, State Of
- Anahaim
- Berkeley
- Brulinigame
- El Cerrito
- El Sobrante
- Fairfield
- Hercules
- Inglewood
- Long Beach
- Los Angeles
- Oakland
- Pinole
- Sacramento
- San Francisco

Cemeteries
- Carver Memorial Cemetery
- Inglewood Cemetery
- Rolling Hills Memorial Park
- Sunset View Cemetery

Churches
- Apostolic Temple Of Truth

- Ark Of Jesus Holiness
- Bethel Temple Pentecostal
- Church Of Deliverance
- Elisabeth Missionary Baptist
- Faith Tabernacle A.O.H. Church Of God
- Gloryland Apostolic Cathedral
- Greater Faith Pentecostal
- New Beginnings Ministry Of Love
- New Beginnings Spiritual Hospital
- North Richmond Missionary Baptist
- Now Faith Church Of God In Christ
- Sunset Missionary Baptist

College
- Contra Costa College

Contra Costa County
- Animal Services
- Courthouse
- Martinez
- Richmond

Countries
- China
- Germany, East
- Germany, West
- Iran
- Iraq
- Soviet Union
- United States

Daniel
- Roosevelt

Diseases
- AIDS

- Alzheimer's
- Diabetics

Dukakis
- Michael

Earthquake
- Loma Piretta

Elections
- 1980
- 1984
- 1988
- 1992

Exxon
- Valdez

Freeway
- Cypress

Gorbachev
- Milkail

Graduations
- Class Of 1992
- Class Of 1994

Haley
- Alex

Hotel
- Golden Nugget

Hospitals
- Brookside

Doctor's

- Kaiser
- Richmond

Jackson
- Janet
- Jesse
- Michael

Kennedy
- Edward

King
- Coretta
- Martin Luther, Jr.
- Martin Luther, Sr.

LaBelle
- Patti

Mandela
- Nelson

Marshall
- Thurgood

Mortuaries
- Angelus
- Benevolent
- Fuller's
- Sunset View

Nevada, State Of
- Reno

Newspaper
- West County Times

Olympics
- 1984
- 1988
- 1992

Organization
- Shepherd Way

Perot
- Ross

Political Parties
- Democratic
- Republican

Robinson
- Julius

Ross
- Diana

Schools
- Adams Middle
- DeAnza high
- Ellerhorst Elementary
- Fairfield High School
- John F. Kennedy High
- Knolls Learning Center
- Nystrom Elementary
- Sheldon Elementary
- Valley View Elementary

Space Exploring
- Galileo
- Magallen
- Voyager I

- Voyager II

Space Shuttle
- Atlantis
- Challenger
- Columbia

Texas, State Of
- Dallas/Ft. Worth
- Waco

United States Presidents
- Bush, George
- Carter, Jimmy
- Clinton, Bill
- Johnson, Lyndon
- Reagan, Ronald

Wedding
- James & Belinda Birdsong

Wonder
- Stevie

About the Author

It was told to James Birdsong, Jr. every since he was born that he was going to be somebody very special in life. James mother have always told him that he is a "professor" and that he is very brilliant and smart. She also encouraged her son to continue to stay with the Lord and he will be blessed. In other words, this is a advice that he followed for many years starting from a baby.

James is a native of the San Francisco Bay Area. He was born in the Bay Area city of Richmond, CA on May 16th, 1980 to James C. Birdsong, Sr. and Belinda Germany Birdsong. His mother named their son James Charles Birdsong, Jr. after his father. He comes from a very popular, well known family that consists of preachers, singers, teachers and entrepreneurs.

A special blessing came in James life when he was only three years old. This was the time that he have received his calling into the ministry to preached the gospel of Jesus Christ after he was healed from a speech impairment. In otherwords, he could not opened his mouth to say a word.

James have preached his first real sermon in a church service when he was fifteen years old when he returned to his native town to spend a weekend with his father. The sermon was brought forth at Holy Mission Christian Center Church of God In Christ during Sunday morning services. James and his father first joined this church when he was ten years old, and where he was baptized

Growing up in the 1980's and 1990's, James have witness many things that made major headlines such as the Iraq/Iran War from 1980 to 1988, the Cold War between the United States and Russia (the former Soviet Union) through 1990 after World War II ended in 1945, the 1992 L.A. Riots that made headlines in Los Angeles after the 1991L.A. Police beating of Rodney King, Martin Luther King, Jr's birthday taking effect as a national holiday, Michael Jackson's album Thriller making news as the best selling album of all time and the 1989 Loma Prietta Earthquake that hit through out the San Francisco Bay Area, which James remembers.

James parents were very active in the ministry and the entire community during the middle and late 1980's such as establishing and operating a food pantry from their home and a local church that made headlines in the West County Newspaper. This presented his parents with a award from the former mayor of Richmond George Livingston in 1988 for their commitment to the community.

But it was in James early teens that have became a time of many trials and hardships such as his parents marriage going to a downfall, wanting to take his life, going home with bad grades, him and his mother moving to Fairfield, CA (where they now reside), his father losing his eyesight in his late teens, & the death of his father in 1997 that have inspired him with the help and the leading of the Lord to write this autobiography at the age of fourteen.

The Lord indeed have truly brought James from a mighty long way. James was presented with the Award of Honor in 1998 during his senior year at Fairfield High School at their annual senior award ceremony and reception. This made James the only Fairfield High School senior out of the entire 1998 graduating class that was presented with the Award of Honor.

James is a member of the Fairfield/Suisun affiliated chapter of the National Alliance of Black School Educators in Fairfield a community worker in the Fairfield area as well as the entire Solano County area for the African American community and in education, given the title "The Pastor of Fairfield High School" while in high school and many other accomplishments.

In 1999, James had the honor to be the Master of Ceremony at the 10th Annual Booker T. Washington Revisited Student Conference, which was held at Solano Community College. He is a evangelist that is now an author that have wrote two books. He is working on establishing a business in the gospel music industry in promoting concerts and plays in the Fairfield and Oakland area along with his mother. James plans to do a gospel album to this autobiography and write a screen play that will become a movie by the year 2000.

Printed in the United Kingdom
by Lightning Source UK Ltd.
9833700001BA